"Sweet Adversity"

The Story of First Kilraughts Presbyterian Church
1971-2010

By
S. ALEX. BLAIR, M.A.

Being a companion volume with
"KILRAUGHTS: A KIRK AND ITS PEOPLE"
which recorded the congregation's history
1660-1971

Published 2010
by the Committee of First Kilraughts
Presbyterian Church

ISBN: 978 1 906689 26 1

Printed by
Impact Printing, Coleraine & Ballycastle

CONTENTS

**"Sweet are the uses of adversity
Which, like the toad, ugly and venomous,
Wears yet a precious jewel in his head."**

"As You Like It" by William Shakespeare

Quoted by the Rev. J. McConnell Auld, M.A., when he preached in the new First Kilraughts Church on Sunday, 29th June 1975.

He said the congregation understood well what Shakespeare was saying and the quotation has become the inspiration for the title of this book.

FOREWORD

By

The Rev. Noel McClean, B.Sc., Dip.Th.

In 1973 just after the fire in First Kilraughts, Mr. Alex Blair undertook the task of writing a congregational history which was entitled "A Kirk and Its People". It is now out of print and those who still have their copy treasure it very much – since it not only tells the story of the congregation but also gives a valuable insight into the history of the entire district of Kilraughts and shows how its people have influenced life in this part of North Antrim.

Now in 2010 the congregation is celebrating the 350th anniversary of the ordination of the first minister. Various celebrations have been planned both spiritual and social. It seemed right that the history book should be updated and once again the most obvious person to do this was Alex. Blair. Since the first book was published in 1973, Mr. Blair has written numerous other books and must be fully conversant now with almost every church in the district. We thank him for his willingness again to commit to writing the recent story of the congregation that he loves the most. The reader will immediately sense the attention to detail which the author gives to this book. The title "Sweet Adversity" has changed from the original but it is still the story of the Kirk and its people.

Like all that happens in a church, many people's talents are involved. Sincere thanks to Alex. and also to all who have been involved in this mammoth task. It is my hope that by reading this volume you will be inspired by the story that unfolds and with us, in our celebration year, give thanks to God who changes not as the years go by.

May the church that has borne witness to the Christian faith for the past 350 years continue to flourish and bring Glory to God in the years and in the generations yet to be.

AUTHOR'S PREFACE

The fire which destroyed First Kilraughts Presbyterian Church building on Palm Sunday, 4th April, 1971, proved a definitive moment in the congregation's long history.

"Kilraughts: A Kirk And Its People" told the story to that date and now I have lived long enough to write a second book outlining events from 1971 to 2010, the 350th Anniversary of the congregation's foundation.

It is unusual to write about an entire period through which one has lived, but this is the case here. The events are all fairly recent and some happened only a few months ago, so this is not truly history. It is merely a record of events of the last forty years but I hope it is a worthy record written by one who was there. In such a situation there is always the possibility of bias and misinterpretation but I have tried to be as accurate and balanced as I can.

I send this book out, knowing it has its imperfections, but recognising that if it makes half the impact which the first one did, I will be well satisfied.

1st September, 2010.

S. Alex. Blair

AUTHOR'S THANKS

Many people have helped me in the writing of this book and to all of them I am most grateful.

The Rev. Noel McClean initiated the project and has given it enthusiastic support throughout. I appreciate his interest and thank him for the Foreword which he has written.

The members of Committee were prepared to shoulder the financial responsibilities which such a publication presents and I am grateful to them.

Members of the congregation and leaders of organisations kindly provided photographs and information and their contributions have been invaluable.

The photographs of organisations in 2010 were taken by Mrs. Vanda McClure and Mr. Stephen McClelland. They gave much time to ensure these were all of the highest standard and they have earned our thanks and congratulations.

Mrs. Nora Workman bravely undertook the task of typing my manuscript. In this she showed endless patience, attention to detail and good humour. Meticulous and most conscientious, I owe her a very special and personal word of thanks.

I am indebted to Impact Printing for their work on this book and I would like to thank Mr. Tommy McDonald, Mr. Peter McCaughan and especially Mr. Nigel Johnston. He designed the cover, which encapsulates so dramatically an unforgettable image from the recent history of First Kilraughts, and has seen the book through all its stages with consummate professionalism and skill.

My grateful thanks to him and to all the other staff, as well as all who have been in any way involved.

1st September, 2010.

S. Alex. Blair

The Chi-Rho Stone at Drumaquern

The ruins of the Medieval Church of Kilraughts which was repaired for the Planters and from which the Rev. Wm. Cuming was ejected in 1661

Chapter 1

FROM THE FOUNDATION TO THE FIRE
- MORE THAN THREE HUNDRED YEARS
OF HISTORY

An ancient standing stone on the side of a disused laneway at Drumaquern in the parish of Kilraughts is a reminder of the early days of Christianity in the area. The stone is inscribed in monogram form within a circle with the "chi" and "rho", the first two letters of the name "Christ" in Greek. Called by the locals "Old Patrick" and said to denote a visit by the patron saint, it obviously goes back to the period of the Celtic Church. Even if it is not as early as Patrician times, it can be dated to the seventh or eighth centuries, and was the fore-runner of the more famous Celtic crosses. What makes it so special for archaeologists and historians is the fact that, on the opposite side, is the reversed rho, unknown in stones anywhere else in the country.

On the hillside above it is another early Christian link in the townland named Knockanavery, which means "The Mass Hill" and not far away is a more obvious Christian site. In the town land of Kilraughts are the remains of an early church building. This church is mentioned in martyrologies of the seventh and twelfth centuries and in the Taxation of Pope Nicholas IV, 1306, where it was valued at half a mark. In the Middle Ages the church was under the care of the monks of the Benedictine Abbey of the Holy Trinity of Down, Downpatrick.

At the Reformation, it became a Protestant church under the Church of Ireland. The Charter of Connor, 1609, placed Kilraughts and seven other parishes in the corps or union of the Prebend of Rasharkin. This covered a wide area of Co. Antrim and Kilraughts was one of the weakest elements in the union. The church building fell into disrepair and by 1622 was described as "decayed". A note in the Ulster Visitation Book of that year stated: "No church nor able to maintain any, the people resort to the next church". In 1622 Kilraughts is called a grange and we are told:

> "The second part of all tithes are impropriate to the Abbey of Down and possessed by the Earl of Antrim. The third part of the tithes belong to Mr. Dunbar, Prebend."[1]

A few years later, the situation had changed. In a letter written from Ballycastle, dated 27th April 1631, the landlord, Sir Randal MacDonnell, Earl of Antrim, wrote to the Church of Ireland Primate, Dr. James Usher, saying that he was doing his best to repair churches on his lands. His letter included this passage:

> "This year I propose to work at the destroyed church of Kilraughts, but the rector, Robert Dunbar, though a man of £100 a year, will only pay 40 shillings towards it. I think you should write to Dunbar".

SCOTTISH PLANTATION AND FIRST MINISTER

It would appear that repairs were carried out, probably at the Earl's sole expense, for he was anxious to have churches available for the settlers he was bringing in from Scotland. This was MacDonnell's private plantation and Lowland Scots were taking up residence in farms in the Kilraughts area. They were Presbyterians and soon were in sufficient numbers to call their own Scottish Presbyterian minister to conduct worship in the repaired parish church. The man they called was the Rev. William Cuming, M.A., from Morayshire, a graduate of King's College in the University of Aberdeen, and he arrived in 1660. The Presbyterian congregation, now known as First Kilraughts, takes this date as its date of foundation.

At first there was no objection to Presbyterian ministers officiating and being paid the tithe in the Church of Ireland. They were known as "Prescopalians" and it was said they brought an academic standing and prestige to the embryonic

Church of Ireland which it greatly needed.

However, with the Restoration of the King in 1660 and the appointment of Bishop Jeremy Tayor to Down and Conor, a clamp-down took place. The Act of Conformity was strictly enforced and this made it clear that all ministers functioning in parish churches must accept Episcopacy and the Anglican Prayer Book or be ejected. Mr. Cuming, like many others, chose ejection.

It is said that on the Sunday after he left, the sexton opened the church door but retired, leaving the key in the lock. A clergyman who had conformed arrived to conduct worship but, when he entered he saw the carcasses of two sheep suspended from the roof beams. There was no congregation and the church building had been defiled. A service was never held there again but the graveyard was used for many years by the Presbyterian settlers and is still occasionally used today.

Mr. Cuming retired to a farm at Toberbilly, which his family held, and he conducted worship in a barn there and in various other places in the area. He died in Kilraughts in 1671.

FIRST MEETINGHOUSE

After his death it is said the people gathered for worship on the leaward side of the hill of Carnageeragh and about 1690 they erected their first primitive meetinghouse in the adjacent townland of Kilmoyangie. Here the Rev. Robert Neilson, a Tyrone man, who had worked as a probationer in the Laggan Presbytery in Donegal, was ordained in 1698. He was provided with a house and farm in 1704 but the people brought charges against him and did not pay his stipend. The Synod ordered them to "pay up" and Mr. Neilson, "more out of regard for the people's good than upon any just fault proved against him,"[2] said he would resign as soon as he received the three years' stipend due to him, which amounted to £60. At the Synod of

1714 it was reported that Mr. Neilson's money had been paid and he had demitted the charge. He lived on in the Kilraughts area and died there in 12th May 1721.

The addition of some townlands formerly belonging to Ballymoney improved the financial position of Kilraughts congregation and enabled the people to call the Rev. John Cochrane as their next minister. He came from Ramoan and was ordained in Kilraughts on 27th September 1716. During his ministry a much larger meetinghouse was erected in the townland of Carnageeragh, which has been the church site ever since. Mr. Cochrane involved himself in many of the controversies of the time, being a firm supporter of Subscription to the Westminster Confession of Faith and a strong opponent of the Seceders. He was Moderator of the Synod of Ulster in 1738 and Clerk of the Synod from 1741-1758. In 1748 he left Kilraughts to become minister of Bangor.

The Rev. Robert Ewing was his successor. A native of the Kilrea area, he had gained some fame in his early years as a boxer. He was ordained in Kilraughts on 12th June 1751 and during his ministry the congregation of Armoy was established with Mr. Ewing's support. He died on 23rd September 1786 at Checker Hall and his headstone, built into the wall of the old ruined church of Kilraughts, is the earliest legible one to be found there.

After a vacancy of over three years, the Rev. Matthew Elder from near Garvagh became the next minister. He lived through the troubled times of the United Irishmen's Rebellion of 1798 in which many of his congregation were involved and saw the rebel forces encamped on the hill of Carnageeragh, just above the meetinghouse. However he distanced himself from these activities, which did little for his popularity amongst the members of the congregation. He was put in the ignominious position of having to collect his own stipend for the first twenty-eight

Headstone of the Rev. Robert Ewing, minister 1751 – 1786, built into the wall of the ruined church in Kilraughts Old Churchyard

years of his ministry but in 1818 Mr. Alexander McIlhatton was appointed stipend collector of the congregation. He was given a "cut" of £3 on every £50 he collected.

FIRST MINUTE BOOK

The first extant Kirk Session Minute Book is from this period and shows that, in the days before a Welfare State, the church was the only support of the poor in times of difficulty, especially when a death took place. An indication of this is given in some extracts from this Minute Book:

"27th May, 1816
To James Moore's Bill for making poor woman's coffin   12/6
To Wm. Cristy's Bill for the same   6/-

30th March, 1817
To Weeda Bredy for the burial charges of her mother   4/8
To Joseph Ronylds for burying a poor man   2/10

3rd May, 1818
To the Sexton for firing in the Session House   3/4
To Wm. Reid and John Carson for a poor woman's coffin   5/-"
To Jean Smiley's coffin   5/-

The two Communion Seasons of May and November were always the highlights of the year for Kilraughts Presbyterians and some of the bills for "Sacramental Expenses" for the period 1816-1837 still survive and reveal interesting details. The sacramental wine was purchased in a public house in Ballymoney. The names of publicans mentioned include William Neal, James Moore and James Gamble. They supplied usually between five and seven gallons of port wine and a gallon or a gallon and a half of spirits. James Gamble and Jean Gamble are mentioned as being the suppliers of the Communion Bread which is sometimes termed "wasels" or little cakes. Usually about six dozen wasels were supplied. Other purchases included nails, pins and inkle and these were used for fixing the linen cloths put over the tables. The word "inkle" is listed in the Oxford English Dictionary as meaning "a kind of linen tape."

The elements (that is the bread and wine) were brought from Ballymoney by dray cart on the Saturday afternoon before Communion and stored in the house of Sarah Cole, where some members of Session gathered to sit with them through the night. During that night the spirits were consumed and after the Communion service the Session met to make sure all was in order and that no wine or spirits remained. These were the days before temperance or total abstinence came into prominence in the Irish Presbyterian Church. Drink was given and taken generously at births, weddings and funerals as well as to the minister in virtually every house during his visitation. It was said that Mr. Elder "had" only two prayers. These he committed to memory and used alternatively but the story is told that, after a day's visitation and partaking of the generous hospitality of his people, Mr. Elder found great difficulty in collecting his thoughts sufficiently to be able to deliver either of them!

CHURCH RE-BUILT

The Rev. Matthew Elder inaugurated a great re-building scheme at the meetinghouse in 1819 which resulted in an impressive building. It is described in the Ordnance Survey Memoir for the parish, written in 1837, as being "very large and capable of holding from eight hundred to one thousand persons". It was rectangular in shape with the pulpit in the centre of the long wall. There were galleries on the two wings and on the other long wall facing the pulpit. The aisles were wide and

First Kilraughts Church building which was in use from 1820 to 1892

here the tables were placed for the communion services. On the ground floor new pews were installed but in the galleries the best of the pews from the old church were re-erected. There were three entrance doors, one in each gable and one in the middle of the long wall opposite the pulpit. These doors gave access to the three aisles. Two rows of short windows provided ample light and the roof was slated. Regarded as the biggest meetinghouse in the entire district, it was familiarly known as "Big Kilraughts", a title which survives today. The O.S. Memoir states that it was "neat in appearance and comfortably fitted up internally." The dimensions of the building are given as 74 feet long by 36 feet wide and the total cost of its erection was £700.

The whole re-building scheme was not completed until 1822 when the bills were finally settled for the finishing of the Session house. Kilraughts church then had a set of fine buildings with a surrounding green area termed a "park". This eventually became the graveyard but at this time all interments were still taking place in the Old Churchyard at Kilraughts.

The Rev. Matthew Elder died at Pine Hill on 23rd January 1827 and was buried in Kilraughts Old Churchyard. His tombstone there declares that:

> "He faithfully preached a Crucified Christ is the only foundation of the believer's hope."

He was survived by his wife, formerly Miss Graham of Dunboe and by a large family. One son Thomas emigrated to Australia and his great-granddaughter worshipped in First Kilraughts on 24th June 1990.

In the vacancy which followed the congregation became embroiled in a bitter dispute over the candidature of a young licentiate from Ballymena, William Dool Killen. Some accused him of being an Arian and they seized the keys and locked the doors of the meeting house to prevent him preaching. However, he and his supporters obtained access but in the vote which followed Mr. Killen lost by the narrowest of majorities. He became minister of Raphoe and later Professor and President of the Presbyterian College, Belfast.

Kilraughts was put under a Committee of Synod and this committee reported in 1831 that they had ordained the Rev. Thomas Leslie as minister. He came to a much depleted congregation for more than half the members had left because of the dispute. Some joined the Covenanters giving Kilraughts congregation of that denomination the numerical boost to be recognized as a separate Reformed Presbyterian congregation. Others joined the new Presbyterian 'cause' at Ballyweaney, giving it the strength to acquire congregational status in 1835. Quite a number also joined the Seceders at Magheraboy, later known as Bushvale congregation.

THE REV. THOMAS LESLIE

The Rev. Thomas Leslie has been described as "a most worthy and high-minded young man, too independent to please the Session and not strong enough to curb them".[3] Disputes still seem to have been a regular feature of congregational life and one of the most notorious of these came to be known as "The Jamie Boreland Case".

When Mr. Leslie had been minister in Kilraughts for some time, the Committee decided to increase his stipend. The only way to do this was to add a small percentage to the annual pew rent. Most pew holders co-operated but one named Jamie Boreland refused. As far as Jamie was concerned the sum involved was about two shillings per year but Jamie was quite adamant that he would not pay. A deputation from the church committee called on him to request payment and made it clear that, if the money was not forthcoming, legal proceedings might have to be taken. Jamie retorted by addressing the leader of the deputation, Mr. D. J. Megaw, in words which were remembered

9

throughout North Antrim for generations. He said: "Weel, Davvit John, tae the law ye may go, but it'll be gie hard to prove value received".

When the deputation reported to a meeting of Session and Committee, it was decided not to take legal proceedings but instead to put boards over the part of the pew owned by Boreland. This did not daunt Jamie, who came to church and perched himself on top of the boards. He was then removed from his perch, marched out of the church and escorted on to the road side. He then brought legal proceedings against the committee and the decision of the court was that the committee had overstepped its authority. The committee had the legal right to remove him and put him outside the church door, but no further. The committee lost the case and had to pay £10 costs. Jamie was triumphant! The story goes that Mr. Leslie took the matter so much to heart that soon afterwards he left for the mission field. In fairness to Mr. Leslie, however, it must be stated that he had been seriously contemplating missionary work for some time.

The Rev. Thomas Leslie resigned from the charge of Kilraughts on 27th January 1835 and became what was termed at that time "the first Christian Missionary to the heathen from the Synod of Ulster". At a great service in Fisherwick Church, Belfast, he was commissioned for missionary service, the famous Dr. Henry Cooke giving the charge. On 19th March 1835, accompanied by his wife, their baby daughter and his wife's mother, he sailed for Jamaica. Alas, he died of fever on 18th August, as did his wife's mother. They were both buried in the graveyard at Lucea. His wife and daughter returned to Ireland where the daughter later married a local man named Trolland and spent the rest of her life in the Kilraughts area. She had a number of children, one of whom was named Thomas Leslie Trolland.

Mr Leslie's work and sacrifice made the Synod of Ulster

more aware of the need to send out missionaries and one of the first decisions of the General Assembly, when it was created in 1840, was to send two missionaries to India.

A poem, written in tribute to Mr. Leslie, included the verse:

"Remember thee long shall the friends who have known thee,
Remember thee long shall the poor negro slave;
Till she draw her last breath shall a parent bemoan thee – A widow and orphan long sigh o'er thy grave".[4]

SON OF CONGREGATION AS MINISTER

It was a son of the congregation, the Rev. Robert Love of Love's Corkey, Loughgiel, who became the next minister. He was ordained in Kilraughts on 21st June 1836 and in 1840 was Moderator of the Route Presbytery when the Synod of Ulster and the Seceder Synod came together to become the General Assembly of the Presbyterian Church in Ireland. Kilraughts was designated First Kilraughts and the Seceder congregation within the parish at Magheraboy became Second Kilraughts, later Bushvale.

When Dunloy congregation was established, Kilraughts lost some members who found it more convenient to attend worship there. Mr. Love understood this and indeed was one of the specially-invited collectors at the opening of Dunloy church on the 21st August 1842. He lived through the dark days of the Potato Famine and had a very close relationship with his people, for he was one of them. Meticulous and conscientious, he kept accurate records of baptisms and marriages and it was during his ministry that the graveyard at the meetinghouse came into use. It was in that graveyard that he was buried when he died very suddenly on the 18th January 1849 aged 36 years. The impressive headstone erected at his grave declared that "God has taken away the flower in youth to plant and water it in the garden of Heaven".

Later Mr. Love's brother and sisters left a house and farm at Breckagh for use of the congregation as a manse. The gift was in memory of the Rev. Robert Love.

Mr. Love's successor was the Rev. Samuel Finlay from Kilcranny, Coleraine, ordained in First Kilraughts on 12th March 1850. Greatly beloved and highly esteemed for his ability as a preacher and for the constancy of his pastoral care of the people, Mr. Finlay also took part in many of the meetings held locally during the 1859 Revival. He was a leader in the Tenant Right Campaign, inaugurated Sabbath School Fetes in the congregation and was a strong advocate of education for young people. He encouraged the young to go to college and university

The Rev. Samuel Finlay, minister 1850 to 1887

The Rev. John McCammon, B.A., minister 1887 to 1930

and many ministers and people of note were produced during his time in Kilraughts. Nearly every family had a son named after him, such was the respect in which he was held.

He preached his last sermon on Sunday 22nd March 1885 using the words of Acts 20, 25-27 as his text: "And now behold I know that ye all, among whom I have gone preaching the kingdom of God, shall see my face no more. Wherefore I take you to record this day that I am pure from the blood of all men. For I have not shunned to declare unto you all the counsel of God".

One who was present wrote:

> "The congregation was very still and many were in tears for all knew, and all believed he knew too, that it was his last sermon".

After two years of illness, he died on 12th December 1887 and was buried in the graveyard in a plot selected by himself in front of his pulpit and a short distance therefrom. The congregation later erected a tall obelisk of polished Aberdeen granite over his grave. He left his house and farm at Pinehill to First Kilraughts for use as a manse and also left £1,000 to the congregation.

The Rev. John McCammon, B.A., from Moygannon House near Donacloney was ordained as Mr. Finlay's successor on 8th March 1887. Noted as a most eloquent and evangelistic preacher, he held the charge for 42 years until his retirement on 5th November 1929.

At his Ordination Soiree, held in the church and attended by one thousand one hundred people, one of the galleries, packed to overflowing, began to leave the wall and it was feared it might collapse on top of those on the ground floor. One who was present said "it swayed a bit but people sat their ground and no accident took place". However, it was clear that something must be done to improve the condition of the old building. This was Mr. McCammon's first task in Kilraughts.

CHURCH COMPLETELY RE-DESIGNED AND REFURBISHED

An architect from the firm of Messrs. Young and McKenzie, Belfast, was brought to inspect the property and advise about the alterations and renovations necessary. His plan was for a completely redesigned church and this was accepted unanimously by the congregational committee. The tender of £854 4s. 0d. from the firm of R. & J. Young, Market Street, Ballymoney, was approved and the work was to start in the Spring of 1892. The final service in the old meetinghouse was a Communion Service held on 13th March, 1892, a photograph of the old building was taken (a hundred of these were sold at 6d. each to members), the congregation moved out and the contractors took over.

A description of the work carried out gave these details:

"The old floor has been removed and replaced with heavy well-joined boarding, with suitable ventilators. From the ground floor and gallery the old pews have been removed and replaced with new pews of pitch pine, varnished. Formerly the entrance was by three doors, with the pulpit on the south side. There is now only one entrance at the end facing the main road, and the pulpit is changed to the opposite end. The ground floor is occupied with four rows of pews, the middle now being double, with two large aisles. The gallery is parallel with the pews in the centre of the building, but at the east and west ends it is semi-circular. The front of the gallery is panelled and has a heavy cornice. The ceiling is panelled in deal, varnished, and sheeted diagonally, having heavy moulding between panels. Instead of two rows of short windows on each side as formerly, there is now one row of long windows on each side, of graceful proportions, with lead lights filled with cathedral glass in four tints artistically arranged.

At the entrance has been built a neat porch with flat roof, parapet and moulded cornice. The doorway has a very neat cornice and pediment with trusses. At the other end has been built a minister's room, underneath which is the heating chamber supplied with the boiler and hot water apparatus by which the whole building is heated. The old spouting has been removed and replaced with a large moulded gutter which gives the outside a more effective aspect. It may also be observed that there is a beautiful cut stone wheel window in the entrance gable above the porch, glazed with stained glass"[5]

The church was re-opened on Sunday, 9th October 1892 when the special preacher was the Very Rev. Dr. A. McCaw, senior minister of the Presbyterian Church of Jersey in the Channel Islands and a former Moderator and Clerk of the English Presbyterian Synod.

The building was essentially a new building – nothing but the old walls remained. People were much impressed, as this editorial from "The Ballymoney Free Press" indicated:

"All who knew what the old church was, and had the privilege of being present last Sabbath were struck with the wonderful transformation, and the vast improvement that has been made. Everyone was pleased with the comfort, the commodiousness and the appearance of the house. Everything about it is plain, chaste and substantial, and quite in keeping with the character of the people who are to worship in it from Sabbath to Sabbath. It seems a model of what a Christian sanctuary ought to be…. We congratulate the minister, the session and committee of First Kilraughts on what they have accomplished and hope that in a short time they will owe no man anything".[6]

The re-modelled First Kilraughts Church of 1892 which remained the congregation's place of worship until destroyed by fire on 4th April, 1971

The Breckagh Manse, first occupied by the Rev. John McCammon in 1902

First Kilraughts, when Mr. McCammon became minister, was in the fortunate position of having two manses – Pine Hill, the gift of the Rev. Samuel Finlay and Breckagh, the gift of the Love family. However, it soon emerged that if the Breckagh house and farm were not occupied, the property would pass to the nearest living relative of the Love family. It was therefore decided to sell Pine Hill to the Reformed Presbyterian Church in Kilraughts for a manse and use Breckagh as First Kilraughts Manse.

Breckagh was subsequently renovated, re-modelled and enlarged with new front reception rooms and when completed it was said the house was virtually a reproduction of Mr. McCammon's old home at Moygannon House, near Donacloney. The work began in 1895 and was not finished until about 1904.

The Rev. John McCammon was known for his pulpit oratory and a favourite topic was the Second Coming of our Lord. He was also a most enthusiastic advocate of missions and missionary givings increased six fold during his time in First Kilraughts. Indeed the congregation's contributions to the Foreign Misson were, for many years, the largest made by any rural congregation of the General Assembly. He was also a strong advocate of temperance and was most assiduous in his visitation of the people and in catechising the young. His last appeal, written from his death bed, was an appeal to the people to support the Foreign Mission. He died at Breckagh Manse on 6th February 1930 and was buried in First Kilraughts Churchyard. He was survived by his three daughters, his wife having pre-deceased him.

It was said of him that in the history of First Kilraughts...

"He stands fearless, stern and strict, but his earnest approach and the eloquence of his preaching made him a force to be reckoned with in North Antrim in his day."[7]

17

The Rev. Francis Alexander Robinson, B.A., a native of Belfast, became the next minister. He was ordained on 28th May 1930 and this started a great period of change in the congregation.

A PERIOD OF CHANGE

The provision of a church hall or Lecture Hall, as it was termed, had been talked about for a long time, and Mr. Robinson decided this would be his first big project in the congregation. The old and new session houses and the lower stables were demolished to make way for the new building, which cost £1,729. It was opened on 31st October 1933 by Mrs. R.D. Megaw, Belfast, wife of Mr. Justice Megaw, one of the illustrious Megaws of Ballyboyland. The dedication was performed by the Rt. Rev. Dr. William Corkey, Moderator of the General Assembly and the first event held in the new hall was a reception for Mr. & Mrs Robinson when they returned to Kilraughts after their marriage.

Other changes in the early years of Mr. Robinson's ministry included the provision of the church's first car park; the introduction of individual communion cups; the dedication of the first organ in memory of the Rev. John McCammon; the singing of paraphrases and hymns and the presentation of robes to the minister. None of these developments took place without opposition but Mr. Robinson's ready wit, beaming smile and astute diplomacy diffused many difficult situations. He retired on 31st December 1970 having completed 40 years and seven months as minister of First Kilraughts. (See chapter 4).

THE FIRE, 4th APRIL, 1971

Just after Mr. Robinson's retirement, the church was burned in a massive accidental fire on the morning of Palm Sunday, 4th April 1971. It was due to an electrical fault and, at its height, the flames, leaping hundreds of feet into the air, could be seen over

Group photographed in front of the Old Session House at the Ordination and Installation of the Rev. F.A. Robinson, B.A., 28th May, 1930. Included (left to right): Mr. James McCammon, the Rev. Robert McCammon, Lecumpher (both brothers of the Rev. John McCammon), the Rev. Samuel Wallace, Drumreagh, Clerk of Presbytery; the Rev. Dr. H.C. Waddell, Trinity, Ballymoney; the Rev. F.A. Robinson; the Rev. Alexander H. Dill, First Ballymoney; the Rev. A.P. Black, Castleton, Belfast; the Rev. Alexander Crothers, Roseyards and the Rev. J.C. Culbert, Ballycastle

The Church Hall (now named the Robinson Hall) as it neared completion in 1933

Group at the retirement presentation to the Rev. F.A. Robinson, 25th March, 1971. Included (left to right): Front row – Mr. Frank Robinson. the Rev. F.A. Robinson, the Rev. J.G. Leitch, Mrs. Valerie Gillespie, Mr. Richard Robinson. Middle row – Mrs. A. McR. Brown and Miss Jane McQuiston. Back row – Messrs. W.A. Tweed, Wm. Carson, S. Alex. Blair. Howard Gillespie and Robert Patterson

a wide area. The disaster brought messages of sympathy from all denominations and money to help in the rebuilding.

The following notice was inserted in the papers the next week:-

> "The Session and Committee of First Kilraughts Presbyterian Church wish to thank all those who have expressed sympathy with them in the loss they have sustained through the burning of their church, and also to the members of the Fire Brigade, the R.U.C., and those who helped with salvage operations.

People come to look as the flames begin to abate, after the fire,
4th April, 1971

They would like the congregation to know that services are being held in Bushvale Hall until such time as their own Hall is fit for occupation.

Meanwhile they would appeal to all members to rally around them and to be present at worship on Sunday, 11th April, at 12 noon, when the Service will be conducted by the Rev. J. McConnell Auld, M.A., F.R.G.S.

The Sunday School is being discontinued for the Summer."

The book "Kilraughts: A Kirk and Its People" was written as one of many fund-raising efforts for the new church. It gives much greater detail on all the events which have just been outlined in this introductory chapter. Now, as the congregation celebrates its 350th Anniversary, the story is being continued, in detail, in this second book, which brings the history of the congregation up to 2010 and is a companion volume with "Kilraughts: A Kirk and Its People".

The ruined exterior of the Church after the fire, 1971

The burned-out interior of the Church, 1971

Chapter I

1. Ulster Visitation Book, 1622

2. Records of General Synod of Ulster, Vol 1, Pages 302-4

3. W.S. Armour in "The Northern Whig", January, 1927

4. For full poem see "Kilraughts: A Kirk and Its People", S.A. Blair, p.80

5. "Ballymoney Free Press", October 1892. Cutting inserted in Session Book

7. "Kilraughts: A Kirk and Its People", S.A. Blair, p.120

Chapter 2

A NEW MINISTER and A NEW CHURCH BUILDING

With the church building destroyed by fire and the congregation vacant there is no doubt that First Kilraughts had little to commend it to a prospective candidate for the vacancy. Although the people were loyal and generous, it was obvious that the next minister would face a massive challenge and would bear a particularly heavy work-load in the building of a new church. It was no surprise, therefore, that five of the six candidates on the original list withdrew and the one who remained preached but then withdrew also. There were two candidates on a second list and the congregation chose one of these, the Rev. R. McC. Bell, minister of Raphoe and Ballindrait in Donegal, to be the man to lead them at what was a most difficult period in their history.

THE REV. R. McC. BELL, B.A.

Robert McCausland Bell, known as Robin, was a native of Belfast, son of Mr. and Mrs. Samuel Robert Bell. His father was one of the city's most prominent businessmen, head of the firm of S.D. Bell, famous for teas and coffees, and with a number of wholesale and retail premises in the city. Mr. S.R. Bell took a leading part in the public life of Belfast, being a member of the City Corporation and chairman of Belfast Education Committee. The Rev. Robin Bell's mother was formerly Miss Nan Blue, daughter of the illustrious Rev. Dr. Alexander Wylie Blue, one of the personalities of the Presbyterian Church of his day and the esteemed minister of May Street, Belfast, 1916-46. Mr. Bell had two brothers, Alastair and Barry, both in the family business, and a sister, Hilary, for many years rehearsal accompanist to the Royal Ballet in London.

Mrs. Robin Bell was the former Elizabeth Roseanne Dunbar, daughter of Sir Richard and Lady Dunbar, Belfast. She was a physiotherapist and continued to practice when she came to Kilraughts. There were three children – Ann Patricia, who in later years distinguished herself as a nurse in Edinburgh; Hilary Elizabeth Caroline, who became a physiotherapist and married Mr. Essex Havard; and Alexandra Mary who became a member of the teaching staff of Lagan Integrated College, Belfast.

When the Bell family arrived at the Breckagh Manse the girls were only children and they came to a house which had undergone an extensive programme of repairs and refurbishment. It became a place they all grew to love. They enjoyed the country setting with its trees and landscapes and they had a happy family life there, the memories of which the girls still cherish today.

INSTALLATION

Mr. Bell's installation in First Kilraughts took place on Tuesday, 16th November, 1971. The service was held in the Church Hall which had been brought into use again for the Sunday services. It was filled to overflowing with friends from far and near, including many from Donegal, as well as members of First Kilraughts congregation. The Rev. V.G. Corkey, Finvoy, Moderator of Presbytery and Synod, conducted the service and the sermon was preached by the Rev. Harold Boyce, Dervock. The Rev. J.G. Leitch, the Clerk, and convener of the vacancy, read the Rule of Faith and delivered an eloquent charge to minister and people.

Later in the Adair Arms Hotel, Ballymena, the congregation entertained over two hundred guests to lunch. Mr. Corkey presided and the main speech was that of the newly-installed minister, Mr. Bell. Other speakers included the Very Rev. Dr. J.L.M. Haire, Principal of Assembly's College; the Rev. F.A. Robinson, the senior minister; the Rev. Dr. Hugh J. Blair, Ballymoney R.P. church; the Rev. Dr. J H Bewglas, senior minister of Ballindrait; Mr. J.B. McNulty, Clerk of Session,

Left: The Rev. R. McC. Bell with his predecessor, the Rev. F.A. Robinson, at his Installation, 16th November, 1971. Right: Mrs. Ruth E. Robinson greets the Rev. R. McC. Bell after his Installation, 16th November, 1971. Behind is Mr. Bell's sister-in-law, Mrs. Alastair Bell

The Rev. R. McC. Bell meets his new congregation and guests after his Installation Service in the Church Hall, 16th November, 1971

Raphoe; Mr. Charles Russell, Clerk of Session, Ballindrait; Mr. James Robinson, Clerk of Session, First Kilraughts; Mr. J. Boyd Barkley of Kilraughts Y.F.C., and Mr. John Price, an elder in May Street Church, Belfast.

A congregational social was held that night in Bushvale Church Hall. There was a capacity crowd and during the proceedings Mr. Bell addressed the congregation for the first time as minister. Miss Marjorie Gamble presented a bouquet to Mrs. Bell. Mr. W. Arthur Tweed presented a gift to the Rev. J. McC. Auld who had supplied the vacancy, and cheques were presented to the convener, the Rev. J.G. Leitch and Mrs. Leitch by the treasurer, Mr. Robert Patterson. Greetings were conveyed to Mr. & Mrs. Bell and the congregation by Mr. Corkey, the Rev. J.H. Beggs, Toberdoney, and the Rev. Professor F.S. Leahy, Kilraughts R.P. Church. At the conclusion of proceedings, thanks were expressed by Mr. S.A. Blair and Mr. Alastair Bell, brother of the newly-installed minister.

Mr. Bell began his ministry in Kilraughts the following Sunday, 21st November, when he preached an impressive sermon on the text:

> "Also I heard the voice of the Lord saying, whom shall I send, and who will go for us? Then said I, Here am I; send me". (Isaiah 6 v. 8).

It was quite clear he understood the task before him and felt, with the help of Almighty God, he was ready for it. He often recalled that when he drove up to the church on the Sunday morning of his "trial" service, he was greeted by a big notice with the warning "Danger: Keep Out" That was enough to "put off" most people, but not Mr. Bell. He saw it as a challenge and there is no doubt that it was his courage, determination and undaunted spirit which were to prove so essential in the months ahead.

COMMUNION VESSELS AND PULPIT BIBLE DEDICATED

When the church was burned, everything was lost including Pulpit Bible and Communion Vessels. As these were necessary to maintain the ministry of the Word and Sacraments in the hall, suitable substitutes had to be borrowed. When Communion was celebrated the neighbouring churches provided what was necessary and the Family Bible of the Tweed Family of Glennylough was used as a pulpit Bible. However, it was obvious that permanent replacements would be required for the new church. As these could be used also in the hall in the interim period, it was fitting that they should be presented and dedicated before the building of the church. So, on Sunday, 29th October, 1972, Mr. Bell dedicated a silver communion goblet and silver bread plates presented by the Kerr family in memory of Mrs. Kerr's parents, Mr. & Mrs. James Morton, Carnageeragh. He also dedicated trays of communion cups and a portable communion service. On Sunday, 7th January, 1973, he dedicated a new Pulpit Bible, presented by Mrs. Mary A. Davidson, Kilmoyangie.

FUND RAISING EFFORTS

Meanwhile great efforts were being made throughout the congregation to raise money for the building of the new church. A satisfactory insurance settlement resulted in the congregation obtaining £56,190 and the churches of the Route Presbytery, in a retiring collection, taken up in each congregation, raised £974.73p. One of the biggest fund-raising efforts organized within the congregation was the Youth Club's "Grand Auction Sale" held at the church on Saturday, 19th June, 1971. The auctioneers were Mr. Frank McClure, a member of the Youth Club, and Mr. George A. McIlrath, O.B.E., J.P., Kilrea. On that day they sold all sorts of goods which filled the Church Hall and the surrounding yard. These included farm machinery, furniture, antiques, ornaments, household articles and cakes. Many members donated animals and these were sold separately at H.A. McIlrath's sale yard in Kilrea. A total of over £2,000 was raised. Mr. & Mrs. John Matthews organized a special service, Miss Lilian Elliott held a sponsored walk, in which large numbers participated and Mrs. Eileen Dobbin collected a mile of pennies. There were also sales of work, cake sales, fund-raising gatherings in members' homes and Ballymoney Choral Society staged their musical comedy "Vagabond Love" in Bushvale Hall, giving the entire proceeds to the Building Fund.

The present author, Mr. S. Alex Blair, as has already been noted, wrote a history of the congregation entitled "Kilraughts: A Kirk and Its People". When it came on the market it created quite a stir and was heralded as a pioneer of a new kind of detailed church history. Mr. Blair was interviewed on radio and on both B.B.C. and Ulster Television, the interview for U.T.V. being done at the church by Charles Witherspoon, with the new building going up in the background.

The book was reviewed in the local and daily newspapers and aroused much interest all over Northern Ireland. "The News-Letter" said the book was "an everyday story of country folk told superbly"; the "The Belfast Telegraph" regarded it as "a well-told story of a Presbyterian community in which is mirrored the history of our province over the past three hundred years"; the local "Northern Constitution" noted that "much original material is published here which makes this book one of the most important publications to come on the market in recent days" and "The Coleraine Chronicle" regarded it "as of outstanding local interest, very readable and the result of many years of detailed research by the author." The reviewer in the "Journal of Ulster Local Studies" said it was simply "a classic of its kind" and the Rev. Professor Finlay Holmes, in his review in "The Presbyterian Herald" said:

"This is not the external history of a Kirk, it is the internal history of a people, the changing pattern of their lives and customs. The characters and personalities of more than fifteen generations live in incident and anecdote, and their sons and daughters who achieved fame and fortune in business and the professions, without forsaking the values they were given in Kilraughts. Those who want to know what sort of people we are in Ulster, including ourselves, need to read this book." [1]

The books were stored in a room of Mr. and Mrs. William Moore's home at "Seven Acre Hill" and sales were brisk. All profits from the book were given by the author to the Building Fund.

SIGNING THE CONTRACT

The architect, Mr. William Hunter, and his associates were proceeding with plans for the new building. Mr. Hunter was very conscious of the restrictions under which he had to operate. The Church Hall had survived the fire, with some minor damage, and the committee wished to have it repaired and incorporated into the new complex. At a committee meeting, attended by Mr. Hunter, on 9th September 1971, he was asked to provide:-

A church to seat between 400 and 500 people

A session room to double as choir room on Sunday

A room for P.W.A. and church committee meetings to seat approximately 60

A minister's room

A kitchen and store

Cloakrooms and toilets

The site to hold this accommodation was bounded by the church hall, the graveyard and by the building lines on two roadways.

To make the maximum use of space for the church itself, Mr. Hunter chose the shape of a square. Because of the difficulties entailed in roofing a building like this, the corners were cut off and thus the new Kilraughts Church was "born". The church on plan form was to be an octagon with a steel portal frame to support the roof, surmounted by a steel spire finished in glass and copper. Between the church and the hall, the rest of the rooms would be fitted in and the door of the hall would be changed to connect internally with the rest of the building.

Signing the contract for the New Church, 9th May 1973
Seated: Mr. William Cusick, contractor and Mr. W. Arthur Tweed,
congregational secretary. Standing (left to right): Messrs. William Hunter,
Architect, Cyril Blackstock, Quantity Surveyor, Rober Patterson and
William Moore, Joint-Treasurers of the Building Fund and the minister,
the Rev. R. McC. Bell

The committee accepted the plan and put it out to tender. The firm of Alexander Cusick Ltd., Armoy, won the contract and the official signing took place on 9th May 1973 in the offices of R. Robinson & Sons, architects, in Ballymoney. Mr. W. Arthur Tweed, the congregational secretary, signed on behalf of First Kilraughts and Mr. William Cusick represented the main contractors. Others present included the joint treasurers of the Building Fund, Messrs. Robert Patterson and William Moore, who had the responsibility of looking after all the money raised for the new building. Mr. Tweed later commented that the 9th May was a date he would never forget, for with the stroke of a pen, on that morning, he committed the congregation to "a huge task ahead"[2]. It certainly was a solemn if exciting moment. Members saw ahead the prospect of the new building but realised the debt they would have to shoulder and became aware of the massive effort which would be required of them.

The reality of the situation was that the members would have to be responsible for most of the money required and Mr. Bell had given much thought as to how this money should be raised. He was determined that everyone would be involved. On 24th May 1973 he launched his scheme which he set out in a circular to every home. It was entitled "Where do we go from here? – The answer rests with you". He informed the congregation that the contract price was £114,822, but that did not include professional fees and furnishings which would add some £25,000 to the bill. The insurance settlement and money raised so far amounted to £65,000, so the balance to be met would be in the region of £75,000. He planned for this to be paid off in seven years and he had previously asked the congregational committee to take the lead by indicating to him what each intended to contribute. He estimated their total, over seven years, would bring in £22,000, so the remaining £53,000 would rest on the shoulders of the members. Mr. Bell appealed to everyone to play a part and he suggested three different methods of contributing:

33

The site being cleared for the building of the new Church

The steel frame and spire of the new Church take shape

1. Direct Lump Sum Donation

2. Weekly, monthly, half yearly or yearly contributions

3. Covenanted subscriptions using the methods outlined in 2.

He also appealed for any, who could afford to do so, to give the congregation interest-free loans. The response of the people was magnificent. A remarkable number of interest-free loans was offered and all gave to the utmost of their resources. Mr. Bell later said he was humbled and amazed by the generosity of the congregation and went forward knowing that all would work out satisfactory.

On the church site the burned-out walls of the old building had to be demolished and the place cleared. This was accomplished in May 1973 but it was quite a task. The fire revealed that most of the main walls were from the old church of 1820 and they were of stone and built to last. The walls of the 1892 re-modelling were of red brick and easily tumbled but the old walls resisted until special implements had to be used. When the site was ready, the foundations were put in and the great steel girders, which were to constitute the frame of the new church, were erected.

THE FOUNDATION STONE IS LAID

A great boost was given to everyone when the ceremony of the Laying of the Foundation Stone took place. It was held on the afternoon of Saturday, 8th September 1973 and great crowds of visitors and friends joined the congregation for the event.

A large marquee had been erected in a field owned by Mr. J. Richard McClure, Church View, on the opposite side of the Moyan Road from the church site. There the service took place conducted by the Moderator of the Route Presbytery, the Rev. John Mulree, St. James's, Ballymoney. After the singing of the "Old Hundredth" Psalm, Mr. Bell led the congregation in an

The Foundation Stone is laid by the Rt. Rev. Dr. John W. Orr, Moderator of the General Assembly, 8th September, 1973. With him (left to right) are: Mr. Wm. Cusick (main contractor), the Rev. F.A. Robinson, the Rev. John Mulree, Moderator of Presbytery, the Rev. R. McC. Bell, Mr. Wm. Hunter and Mr. David Robinson (architects)

With the shadows of the iron framework around them, the Rev. Dr. Hugh J. Blair, Ballymoney R.P. Church, and Mr. J. Kenneth. C. Armour, son of the famous Rev. J.B. Armour, are photographed after the Laying of the Foundation Stone

The ministers, followed by the congregation, leave the marquee where the service was held to walk across the road to the Church site for the Laying of the Foundation Stone, 8th September, 1973

Mr. William Hunter, who designed the new Church building (left), with the Rev. F.A. Robinson, the Rev. John Mulree and Mr. Wm. Cusick, after the Foundation Stone Laying Ceremony

Although facilities where few, the ladies managed to get afternoon tea to all who attended the Foundation Stone Laying, 1973

Affirmation of the Christian faith and the senior minister, the Rev. F.A. Robinson, offered prayer. The sermon was preached by the Moderator of the General Assembly, the Rt. Rev. Dr. John W. Orr, Bloomfield, Belfast. After the singing of the hymn "This stone to Thee in faith we lay", the ministers processed across the road and into the site of the new building. The people followed and, with the beams of the new church rising round them, the foundation stone of Westmoreland slate was laid by the Moderator of the General Assembly. Afterwards tea was served and, fortunately, the afternoon was sunny and warm, for there were few facilities for accommodating large numbers of people. The hall and nearby stables were utilised but the yard between was also seated and many enjoyed afternoon tea in the open air. It was a memorable and happy day and the members of the congregation were greatly encouraged by the huge numbers who attended. As one visitor put it:

"There is great good-will for Kilraughts in the entire North Antrim community, of all creeds and classes".

As members came each Sunday to morning service they took a keen interest in the progress of the building. Everything went satisfactorily and main and sub-contractors worked hard to have the building completed by May 1975.

THE NEW COMPLEX IS REVEALED

The new complex was revealed as a great gleaming white edifice, a modernistic building, clearly intended to capture the imagination of generations to come. Many who were qualified to judge liked it very much but there were those who were not so impressed. One man said it stood "like a sore thumb sticking up in the midst of a beautiful countryside." He did admit the interior was more attractive.

The main church was octagonal with a graceful copper tipped spire and stood in well-laid-out grounds. On the north side was a neatly designed extension to the graveyard with broad tarmacadam walks giving easy access. On the southern side, across the Moor Road, was a large car park with cement divisions separating the principal parking ranks. Around the church itself there were tarmacadam and grass areas. A feature of the grounds was a Garden of Remembrance featuring archways and a cairn of stones from the old church.

Two sets of double doors in iroko timber and glass gave access to the vestibule where the foundation stone and a stone commemorating the opening and dedication of the building were positioned. The vestibule floor was laid in burnt-clay ceramic tiles in Patrician red. The ancillary rooms led off the vestibule and these included the session room, spacious kitchen and small office. A dramatically designed room here was the Circular Room, laid out to provide maximum participation between audience and speaker and to encourage "togetherness". The

The new building nears completion

ceiling was of parana pine, the walls of Tyrolean plaster and the main furnishings of mahogany. The Circular Room had four plate-glass windows with engraved designs illustrating the 23rd Psalm, chosen for its relevance to a rural and pastoral setting.

The Church Hall, which survived the fire, was also within the complex and had been re-modelled. The balcony, cloakrooms, door and south side windows had been removed and the walls, both interior and exterior, were re-plastered to tone in with the rest of the buildings. A new maple strip floor was laid and new windows installed in the south wall. The McMaster Memorial Windows, which had been presented many years before in memory of Mr. and Mrs. David John McMaster, were inserted in the east wall, directly opposite the place which they had originally occupied. Part of the stage and the stage curtains had been burned in the fire and these were replaced.

The highlight of the whole complex was the church itself, octagonal in shape, with alternate sides projecting in a manner suggestive of a cross. The great steel girders which formed the frame of the building were covered in iroko timber and on top was a steel spire finished in glass and copper. The ceiling was of parana pine sheeting and the walls were of Tyrolean plaster. The pews were arranged in a "gather around" manner with the pulpit and communion table in the centre, together with a lectern and baptismal font. All of these were of mahogany. The choir area was in the north aisle, integrated with the congregation, and here was positioned the Cosgrove pipe organ built by the Irish Organ Company. It was designed as a compact instrument in two units – the organ chamber above the central-aisle doors and a detached stop key console facing the congregation.

One of the most striking features of the church was a series of twelve stained glass windows, all donated by members or friends of the congregation. The windows were made at Caldermac Studios, Belfast, and were in three sets of four, each set portraying a Biblical theme.

*The First Kilraughts Church complex, opened and dedicated,
31st May, 1975*

*The Garden of Remembrance with a cairn of stones from
the previous Church*

Behind the pulpit a set of four depicted "The Six Days of Creation" described in the opening chapter of Genesis. There was an impressive use of deep green and blue with purple for the setting of earth, sea and sky within which the heavenly bodies, living creatures and finally man were all shown. These windows were of a darker tint than the others to be easy on the eyes of the congregation as they focused on the pulpit.

The theme was developed in the second set, placed in the south wall. Here the subject was "The New Creation in Christ Jesus", from 2nd Corinthians 5:17. Beginning with Christ's upbringing at Nazareth, His ministry, death and resurrection, the theme unfolded with the portrayal of the Risen Christ presiding over history and bringing renewal to man's industrial, commercial and agricultural pursuits. The windows featured factory chimneys and combine harvesters and the historical and local relevance of the subject was reflected by the inclusion of a representation of the ancient Chi-Rho stone at Drumaquern.

The third set of windows was in the north wall. They presented the final dramatic consummation of the Salvation Story. The theme was "The Revelation of Christ in Glory", based on the opening chapter of the Book of Revelation. Here was portrayed Christ, who is the First and Last, alive for evermore, judging the churches and the world.

Behind the worshipping congregation, and linking the church with the vestibule, there were two white concrete screens filled with antique glass octagons. The variously coloured octagons were interspersed with small glass squares in rich ruby red. The whole pattern symbolized people of different outlook and belief, nation and race, brought together by the atoning blood of Jesus Christ. The minister's room was positioned adjacent to the church and the minister could enter along any of the three aisles.

The new addition to the Graveyard in 1975
(By 2010 virtually all of these spaces have been taken)

The front of the Church with the Creation Windows

The windows depicting the New Creation in Jesus Christ

Side view of the pulpit and front of the Church

The lighting of the buildings and car-park was a striking feature of the entire work and helped to accentuate the strength and beauty of the whole concept. The heating system was low-pressure with two boilers in an external boiler-house attached to the Stables. Two circuits were installed to provide complete flexibility, either heating church or hall or both.

Mr. Bell gave this message to the congregation as they were about to take possession of the new building:

The Chi-Rho Stone at Drumaquern depicted in one of the windows

"Buildings are designed to perform a particular function. In this instance that function is the worship of Almighty God and the witness of His people to the truth as it is in Jesus Christ. One important feature which helps in worship is that of atmosphere. For some members of the congregation it may not be easy at first to adjust to this new building of the 20th century, when they remember so much of the character and 'spirit' of the building that is gone. But in time we all believe that a bond will be formed between the people and the building. It is said that buildings reflect the people who use them. May this be so in Kilraughts, and may these splendid walls become a base for the unleashing of God's saving power in His world."

OPENING AND DEDICATION

The opening and dedication of the new complex, which cost

in total £160,000, was a big event not just for the congregation but for people all over North Antrim and much further afield. It was the first new church erected in the Presbytery of Route since the early years of the twentieth century and its opening was the last official duty in the moderatorial year of the Rt. Rev. Dr. G. Temple Lundie, minister of First Armagh. It took place on the afternoon of Saturday, 31st May 1975, and more than one thousand two hundred people, of all denominations, were present.

The ceremonies began with a procession of Kirk Session and officiating ministers around the exterior of the building. On arrival at the main entrance doors, Dr. Lundie was presented with a commemorative key by Mr. William Cusick, representing the main contractors, A. Cusick Ltd., Armoy. With Mr. Cusick was the architect Mr. William Hunter and Mr. David T. Robinson of the firm of R Robinson and Sons, architects, and Mr. Cyril Blackstock, representing Blackstock and Dowse, quantity surveyors. With the words "Open to me the gates of righteousness: I will go into them and will praise the Lord", the Moderator proceeded into the building. In the vestibule the Clerk of Session, Mr. Andrew McR. Brown, invited Dr. Lundie to unveil a plaque to commemorate the occasion. It was inscribed:

> "Unveiled by the Rt. Rev. G.T. Lundie, M.A., LL.B., D.D., Moderator of the General Assembly, at the Dedication of the New Church Buildings on the 31st May 1975.
>
> 'To God be the Glory'"

In the church the dedication service began with an Affirmation of the Christian Faith led by the Moderator of the Route Presbytery, the Rev. W.J. Mawhinney, First Ballymoney. Mr. Mawhinney then proceeded to the solemn act of dedication. In the name of the Presbytery, he dedicated the church "for

The members of Kirk Session lead the procession at the Opening and Dedication Ceremony, 31st May, 1975

the worship of God, for the preaching of the Gospel, for the celebration of the Sacraments, for comfort to all who mourn, for strength to those who are tempted, for light to those who seek the way, for the hallowing of family life, for the teaching of the young and for the up-building of all believers."

Dr. Lundie prefaced his sermon with words of congratulation to the minister and people of First Kilraughts. He also congratulated the architect, the builder and all who had worked to create a building which he said, had been designed "with such taste and consideration"[3]. He brought the greetings of the General Assembly to the people of First Kilraughts and said that First Kilraughts was the third new church he had opened in County Antrim during his moderatorial year.

The Moderator, the Rt. Rev. Dr. G.T. Lundie, is presented with a silver key by Mr. William Cusick, the main contractor. With him is Mr. William Hunter, architect of the new building

Referring to the gifts which he was to dedicate, Dr. Lundie said he was pleased to note that a number of the donors were from America. He remarked:

The Moderator, the Rt. Rev. Dr. G.T. Lundie, unveils a commemorative stone in the vestibule. With him is the Rev. R. McC. Bell, the minister

Ministers who took part in the Opening and Dedication Service. Left to right: The Rev. F.A. Robinson, the Rev. A.E. Anderson, the Rt. Rev. Dr. G.T. Lundie, the Rev. R. McC. Bell, the Rev. J.G. Leitch and the Rev. W.J. Mawhinney

"As we approach the two-hundredth anniversary of the founding of the American state, it is a happy thought that so many of those who have gone forth from this place have today remembered their mother church."[4]

Dr. Lundie took as his text:

"Unto Him be glory in the church by Jesus Christ throughout all ages."

Ephesians 4 v 21.

Dr. Lundie said the church was

"...the medium for the revelation of God's glory, the body of Christ and the fullness of Him who filleth all."[5]

He spoke of the glory of the Gospel, the glory of worship, especially in a place so beautiful as this new building, and the glory of fellowship within the church.

Prayer was offered by the Moderator of the Synod of Ballymena and Coleraine, the Rev. A.E. Anderson. The Old Testament reading was by the Rev. F.A. Robinson, senior minister, and the Rev. J.G. Leitch, Clerk of the Route Presbytery, read from the New Testament. The Rev. Robin Bell welcomed the huge congregation which filled the church to overflowing and filled also the vestibule, circular room and church hall.

The choir sang the anthem: "O how amiable are Thy dwellings" with Mr. Ronald Waterman, principal of Knockahollet School, at the organ. Mr. Waterman was deputising for the church organist, Mrs. Betty Caldwell, who was indisposed. The guest organist was Mr. Peter Wilson, Railway Street Church, Lisburn, who gave a recital before the service began.

Tea was served and proceedings continued in the Church Hall, where the Moderator of Presbytery, the Rev. W.J. Mawhinney, presided. Dr. Lundie was presented with a copy of the book "Kilraughts: A Kirk and its People", which had been artistically

Mrs. Roseanne Bell and daughters Patricia, Alexandra and Caroline, with Mrs. G. T. Lundie. Patricia presented a bouquet to Mrs. Lundie

Interior of the new Church filled to capacity for the Opening and Dedication, 31st May, 1975

The author of "Kilraughts: A Kirk and Its People", Mr. S. Alex. Blair, presents a specially-inscribed copy of his book to the `Rt. Rev. Dr. G.T. Lundie

inscribed by Mr. Henry Irwin, Principal of Straidbilly School. The presentation was made by the author, Mr. S. Alex. Blair. Mrs. Lundie was the recipient of a bouquet of flowers presented by Miss Patricia Bell, eldest daughter of Mr. and Mrs. Bell.

Mr. Blair read two telegrams of congratulations which had been received. One came from Mr. and Mrs. Robert Moore, Seattle, U.S.A., both of whom had been brought up in the congregation. The other was from another former member, Mrs. Douglas MacDonald, her husband, son and daughter-in-law from Melfort, Saskatchewan, Canada. Mrs. MacDonald was formerly Miss Jeannie Patton, Kilraughts.

Dr. Lundie concluded proceedings by thanking the congregation for the gifts and saying what a wonderful day it had been and how much he and his wife had enjoyed their visit to Kilraughts. He pronounced the Benediction and afterwards many hundreds of visitors took the opportunity of viewing the new suite of buildings. The offering amounted to over £4,000.

GIFTS DEDICATED

The Moderator, Dr. Lundie, during the service in the church, dedicated many gifts. First there were the gifts which had been presented in the old church and which had perished in the fire. They had been replaced:

Communion Table and Two Chairs
in memory of William and Jane Moore, Lisnisk,
the gift of Hugh, William and Robert Moore.

Baptismal Font
in memory of Rose McIlhatton,
the gift of Margaret McIlhatton.

Lectern
in memory of Jackson Grahame and Ellen Adams,
Culkeerin, and of Mrs. Ellen Clarke, Ballyveely
the gift of Mrs. William Kirkpatrick, Lisboy. Rev. 14:13

Offertory Plates
in memory of James and Mary McQuiston, Ballyveely,
the gift of the McQuiston family.

Praise Boards
in memory of William P. Tweed and Isabella Tweed,
The Mullan,
the gift of Thomas Tweed.

Pulpit Fall
the gift of James and Mary Dobbin

Organ
in memory of the Rev. John McCammon B.A.
Minister of First Kilraughts Presbyterian Church
1887 – 1929
the gift of Vida, Hester and Gertrude McCammon.

Portable Communion Set
in memory of Robert Carson, Knockahollet,
the gift of Ivy and Bertie Carson.

Flower Vase
in memory of John Lyle McClure, Church View,
the gift of Elizabeth L. McClure

Pulpit Hymn Book
the gift of Roberta Moore, Seattle, U.S.A.

Cabinet for Communion Vessels
in memory of James and Margaret Patterson, Drumabest,
the gift of Robert Patterson

Vestibule Table
the gift of Elizabeth L. McClure and James Richard
McClure, Church View.

Electric Clock
in memory of William W.Sayers, Larchfield,
the gift of his father and mother, Mr. and Mrs. Andrew
Sayers, Austin and Anna

Lectern Bible
in memory of Sarah Biggart Wilson, Ballynagashel, who
died 18th July, 1958
the gift of Jane Kirkpatrick Delaney, U.S.A. March 1961.
Phil. 1:23

Book Racks for Pews
in memory of Lieutenant Joseph F. Moore,
missing in action with the American Air Force,
August 1st, 1943
the gift of Robert and Agnes Moore, Seattle, U.S.A.
February 1964.

Tablet
in memory of the Rev. John McCammon B.A.
the gift of the congregation.

Tablet
in gratitude for the lives of those members of the
congregation who died in service of their Sovereign and
Nation in time of war, and of those who served.

Tablet
bearing the names of the ministers of
First Kilraughts Church from 1660 to the present day.

Then he dedicated the gifts to the new church:

Pulpit
in memory of Andrew Austin Sayers J.P. and his mother
Mrs. M.I.W. Sayers,
the gift of the Sayers family, Larchfield.

Sound Amplification System
in memory of James and Marion McClure, Blackhills,
the gift of James and Frank McClure and Elizabeth Wilson.

Door to North-side Aisle
in memory of Samuel and Mary Ann McClure,
Killyrammer,
the gift of the McClure family.

Door to South-side Aisle
in memory of John and Margaret Richmond,
Carnageeragh,
the gift of the Richmond family.

Double Doors to Centre Aisle
in memory of Andrew and Mary McClure,
the gift of James M. and Ethel McClure, Philadelphia,
U.S.A.

STAINED GLASS WINDOWS

Window, the gift of the Morning Sunday School

Window in memory of James and Rachel Taggart,
Kilmoyangie, and of their son, Robert,
the gift of Samuel Taggart, Wanganui, New Zealand.

Two windows in memory of William and Minnie Mathews,
Kilmandil, and of their son, William,
the gift of M. Eileen Mathews.

Window in memory of Thomas McClure J.P. and Elizabeth
L. McClure, Church View,
and of their son, John Lyle,
the gift of James Richard and Margretta McClure.

Window in memory of James and Margaret Patterson,
Drumabest,
the gift of Robert and Annie Patterson.

Window in memory of James Dobbin, Kilraughts,
the gift of the Dobbin and Clyde families.

Window in memory of Frank Kirkpatrick, and of James
and Mary McClure,
the gift of Elizabeth Kirkpatrick, Lisboy.

Window, the gift of the Architects, R. Robinson and Sons,
Ballymoney.

Window, the gift of Blackstock and Dowse, Quantity
Surveyors, Ballymoney.

Window in memory of James Robinson, Ballinaloob,
the gift of Elizabeth Robinson

Window, the gift of the Main Contractors, A. Cusick
(Contractors) Ltd., Armoy.

Screen of Concrete Octagonal Panels with Antique Glass
the gift of Robert and Agnes Moore, Seattle, U.S.A.
in memory of their parents, William and Jane Moore,
Lisnisk, and John and Margretta Reid, Drumaquern.

Brass Bookrest for the Communion Table
in memory of Elizabeth Rodgers Rosborough, formerly of
Legacurry,
the gift of her daughter, Emma F.N.R. Fisher, Pennsylvania,
U.S.A.

Hymnbooks for use of Visitors
in memory of William Christie, Mounthamilton,
the gift of Hubert and Marion Christie.

Fall for Church Lectern
the gift of the Rev. Robin and Mrs. Roseanne Bell.

Flower Vase
the gift of Annie S. Bell, Belfast

Flower Stand
in remembrance of William and Minnie Mathews,
Kilmandil, and of their eldest son William,
donated anonymously.

Flower Stand
in memory of Thomas and Margaret Tweed, The Mullan,
the gift of their daughters Elizabeth H. McClure and Mary
I. Currie.

Table for Offertory Plates
the gift of Jane and James McQuiston, Ballyveely.

Desk and Three chairs for Minister's Room
in memory of James Thompson Reid, Drumaquern,
the gift of Annie M. Reid and Family.

Desk and Chair for Office
in memory of Hugh and Agnes Kirkpatrick, Turnagrove,
the gift of Thomas and James Kirkpatrick

Electric Duplicating Machine
the gift of M. Eileen Mathews

Table for Circular Room
in memory of Thomas and Margaret Tweed, The Mullan,
the gift of William P. and James R. Tweed.

Lectern and Chair for Circular Room
the gift of The Rev. F.A. Robinson B.A., and Mrs. Ruth
Robinson

Clock for Circular Room
in memory of Samuel and Ellen McQ. Clarke, Ballyveely,
the gift of Mrs. William Kirkpatrick, Lisboy.

Four Windows for Circular Room
the gift of First Kilraughts P.W.A.

Curtains and Doors for Circular Room
the gift of the Church Choir

Curtains for Church Hall Platform
the gift of Kilraughts Young Farmers' Club

Doors for the Church Hall
the gift of First Kilraughts Youth Club

Original Oil Painting of former First Kilraughts Church,
the gift of S. Alexander Blair B.A.

Main Entrance Doors
The gift of F. Cogan and D.E. Shackleton, Consulting
Engineers,
Steele Brothers and R. Douglas, Heating and Plumbing
Contractors,
T.A. Richmond, Electrical Contractor
P.J. Boyle, Painting Contractor.

Trees for Church Grounds
the gift of Mrs. F. A. Robinson

TALENT SCHEME

The Northern Bank gave a most generous donation towards the publication of a commemorative booklet for the opening of the new buildings. The Morning Sunday School, as has been listed, presented a window and the children and young people raised all the money for this window themselves. They were most enthusiastic and their enthusiasm was channelled into two main projects, which took place during 1973. They engaged in a Talents Scheme by which each pupil was given £1 to be put to the best use they could. Many unusual and diverse jobs were undertaken from selling ball-point pens to doing baking, needlework and working on the farm. The other project was the selling of a competition sheet entitled "The Presbyterian Churches of Co. Antrim" and these two efforts raised £519.35p, which far exceeded the amount required to pay for the window. The effort was applauded as an outstanding achievement. By using a Biblical idea, the young people showed they wished to be identified with their new church in a very real and practical way.

SERIES OF SPECIAL SERVICES

The day after the official opening was Sunday, 1ˢᵗ June, and on that day there began a series of special services which lasted throughout the month.

The guest preacher at the morning service on 1ˢᵗ June was the Rev. Dr. John F. Park, minister of Stormont Church, Belfast, and amongst the many visitors were the Rt. Hon. Lord MacDermott of Belmont and Lady MacDermott. The lessons were read by Mr. Andrew McR. Brown and Mr. S. Alex. Blair.

Mr. Bell conducted the evening service and in his sermon spoke about Solomon's temple and how Solomon insisted on getting only the best, both in men and materials. Mr. Bell declared:

> "We have put our best into this building. It is a beautiful place. It bears the marks of the craftsman's skill. We have done this believing that only the best is good enough for our great God and for the God of our children and the generations yet unborn"[6].

Speaking of the changing times with uncertainty, tension, apathy and indifference in so many quarters, Mr. Bell said people often had said to him in recent months – what a time to launch a venture like the building of a new church? He and the congregation of First Kilraughts would reply – what an incentive to do great things for Christ. Never was such a thing more needed. Mr. Bell concluded:

> "We believe Christ is leading us forward to a fresh opportunity and a new beginning in the work of His Kingdom. Here, in this church, Christ is speaking to us in sound, in symbol, in design and in beauty. What we have erected is not a monument to our past, but a power-house for the great surge forward – it is the House of our God."[7]

At the evening service the lessons were read by Mrs. Eileen Matthews and Mr. Bob Richmond.

> "It is very fine indeed, a fitting memorial to the past – and what a long and distinguished history this congregation has had. It is an ideal contemporary building in which to worship in the present and a splendid monument for posterity."[8]

That is how the Rev. Professor R. Finlay G. Holmes, Magee Professor of Church History and Systematic Theology at

Assembly's College, described the new First Kilraughts Church when he preached at the morning service on Sunday, 8th June 1975. Professor Holmes added:

> "Too often in the past the church has presented a gloomy image, and we Presbyterians have contributed more than our share in this direction; but the light and colour of this building convey the authentic joy and hope of the Christian faith."9

Professor Holmes said that in coming to Kilraughts he felt in a very real way that he was coming home. It was the congregation of both his mother and father and their families and his two grandfathers, Richard Gregg and Robert Holmes, were elders in First Kilraughts. Amongst those in the large congregation who were welcomed by the Rev. Robin Bell, were Professor Holmes's wife and family, and his mother, Mrs. Sophia Holmes, formerly Miss Sophia Gregg of Magherone (Toberbilly).

The guest preacher at the evening service was the Rev. William A. Finlay, Publications Officer of the General Assembly, and former minister of May Street Church, Belfast. Mr. Finlay said the church stood for truth, beauty and dignity. It was a living and vital fellowship, a community which would redeem society and save society from itself. He said that the church was also the instrument of service in the world. This was what Jesus built His church to be.

Mr. Finlay remarked:

> "It is in service to Christ that we find our fulfillment. We can ask for no greater reward, just as we can seek no higher honour."

Again the minister, Rev. Robin Bell, welcomed a large number of visitors and spoke of his pleasure in having Mr. Finlay present, as May Street was the congregation in which he was brought up. The lessons at the services on that Sunday were read, in the morning by Mr. W. Arthur Tweed and Mr. Bertie Kerr, and in the evening by Miss Sadie Johnston and Mr. James Tweed.

Sunday, 15th June 1975 saw history made in First Kilraughts when a Church of Ireland Bishop preached at morning service. The bishop was the Rt. Rev. Dr. Cuthbert I. Peacocke, retired Bishop of Derry and Raphoe. It was the first time ever an Anglican bishop had spoken in Kilraughts and Bishop Peacocke paid tribute to the "vision, generosity and work" which had made the new church possible and said there was much in Presbyterianism which Church of Ireland people admired. They admired especially what he called "the sturdy independence, the loyalty and the high standard of support" which Presbyterians gave their Church. They also admired the involvement of lay people in the work of the congregation and the Presbyterian concern in matters of public welfare.[10] Bishop Peacocke commented:

"We worship God in different ways and in different traditions. Many are scared at the move for the Churches to get closer together. They fear they will lose something valuable or even their identity. But unity does not mean uniformity. Surely it means living in charity one with another, and sharing where we can in common enterprises."[11]

He said it was good for Presbyterians and members of the Church of Ireland to come to know each other and to be able to speak the truth, as each sees it, in the spirit of Christian love. There were differences, he said, but he went on:

"The really important thing is that we recognize the right of everyone to worship God as they believe in their conscience and live in charity and co-operation with one another for the glory of God's Kingdom."[12]

65

Mr. Bell welcomed Bishop and Mrs. Peacocke and said Bishop Peacocke had been for many years rector of St. Mark's Church, Dundela, Belfast, the parish to which his wife and her family belonged. Mr. Bell conducted both the morning and evening services and at both welcomed large numbers of visitors from far and near. At the evening service the address was given by Miss Mary Angus, deaconess in the chaplains' department of the Royal Victoria Hospital, Belfast. The lessons at the morning service were read by Mr. Robert Patterson and Dr. Marjorie Kirkpatrick, while in the evening the readers were Mrs. Clarke Bashford and Mrs. James McIlhatton.

Sunday, 22nd June 1975 was Young People's Day, the first to be held in the new church. Hundreds of visitors meant that congregations at both services overflowed from the church into the vestibule and the evening service had to be relayed to the Circular Room. The young people of the congregation took a prominent part in both services. A choir of young people led the praise and sang a number of special items. Patricia Bell was the soloist in the morning and Mandy Dowey was the soloist in the evening. Rev. F.A. Robinson was at the organ.

The special preacher at the morning service was the Rev. William Hanna, former minister of Windsor Church, Belfast and minister-elect of St. Johnston and Ballylennon Churches, County Donegal. Mr. Hanna was welcomed by Mr. Andrew McR. Brown, the Clerk of Session, who said Mr. Hanna was well-known in the Kilraughts community, being a native of Ballybradden, Loughgiel, and he had relatives in First Kilraughts congregation. Rev. H. Laurence Henry, minister of High Street Church, Antrim, which had just acquired a new church building, was the guest preacher in the evening. He recalled his close association with the congregation of First Kilraughts, where his grandfather worshipped all his life, and where his father was brought up. Mr. Henry spoke of his admiration for the new church which he described as "quite splendid" and congratulated minister and people on their fine achievement.

The lessons were read by Mary McNeill and Alex Crawford, at the morning service, and in the evening the readers were Helen Dowey and James McClure. Collectors at both services were Barbara Moore, Janet Sayers, Elaine McNeill, Frank McClure, Alan Pinkerton and James Patterson.

The special services concluded on Sunday, 29th June with Communion presided over by the senior minister, the Rev. F.A. Robinson, assisted by Mr. Bell and the elders. The service followed the order used by Mr. Robinson during his forty years' ministry in First Kilraughts and included the reading of the Ten Commandments and the singing of four metrical psalms, beginning with the Old Hundredth and ending with the 103rd to the tune Coleshill. In his sermon Mr. Robinson spoke of the beautiful new church and recalled the old church in which he had officiated for so many years. He said he hoped he might be permitted to think of the old building as "his church." Now there was a new minister and a new church, and he observed that no minister could have had a finer successor than he had in Mr. Bell.

The evening service had as its special preacher the Rev. J. McConnell Auld, a member of the teaching staff of the Royal Belfast Academical Institution. Mr. Auld was the last person to conduct worship in the old church before the tragic fire of 4th April, 1971, and, like Mr. Robinson, he recalled the old building, which, he said, had been finely portrayed in the new church in the oil painting presented by Mr. Alex. Blair. He spoke of the joy he had had during what he termed his "mini ministry" in Kilraughts in 1971 when the congregation was vacant and described the people as a "kind, good, generous and devoted people." He said truly Kilraughts congregation knew what Shakespeare talked about when he wrote:

"Sweet are the uses of adversity, which, like the toad, ugly and venomous, wears yet a precious jewel in his head."

He pointed out that there was always suffering and a sacrifice to get something better. Mr. Auld declared:

"The Old Kilraughts was good, but you have achieved something better, and the best still lies ahead in Christ."[13]

Mr. Auld said he saw the new Kilraughts as a place where people from all over the world would come to worship. Perhaps a folk museum of the story of Presbyterianism might be started, inspirational musical concerts held and displays of painting and other works of art put on. Addressing the people he said:

"You, as a congregation, have in this new building a unique opportunity to present the gospel in modern ways to the travellers of life. You could bring people to your doors from all over the world, and, in Goldsmith's words, 'some may stay to pray.'"[14]

The minister, the Rev. Robin Bell, welcomed a large congregation, many of whom were visitors. The church was packed to capacity, and extra seating had to be provided. In welcoming Mr. Auld, Mr. Bell said he was "a very good friend" of the congregation whose "helpfulness and inspiring leadership" would long be remembered. Mr. Bell went on to pay a tribute to the work of the choir and the organist, Mrs. Betty Caldwell. He said the success of the praise and especially the anthem work during the series of special services had been largely attributable to Mrs. Caldwell's efforts. He was sorry she had been indisposed throughout the Opening and Special services and regretted that she had indicated she did not feel able to resume her work as organist. On behalf of the congregation, Mr. Bell wished Mrs. Caldwell and her husband all good wishes for the future. The organists at the special services had included

Mr. Ronald Waterman and Mr. Howard Gillespie, as well as the senior minister, and Mr. Bell thanked them for coming to help at such short notice.

He then went on to say how much the congregation appreciated the skill and work of those principally involved in the erection of the new church buildings and continued:

> "We can do this in an informed way today because we know from the experience of the past month what splendid accommodation has been provided here, and comments about it have been coming in from very many quarters. So, I wish now to place on record the congregation's sense of indebtedness to and appreciation of our architect, Mr. William Hunter, and the firm of R. Robinson & Sons; our main contractor, Mr. William Cusick, and the firm of Alexander Cusick (Contractors) Ltd., Armoy; our quantity surveyor, Mr. Cyril Blackstock, and the firm of Blackstock and Dowse, Ballymoney; and our consultant engineers, Messrs. Shackleton and Cogen, by whose united labours this wonderful work has been accomplished.
>
> I wish also to express the congregation's thanks to the very many sub-contractors and team of workers, all of whom worked cheerfully and harmoniously throughout the duration of the contract. We offer our sincere thanks to them all."[15]

The guest soloist at the evening service was Mr. William Thompson (tenor), conductor of the Ballyclare Male Voice Choir. The lessons at the evening service were read by Mrs. Janette Reid and Mr. Arnold McClure.

The Rev. McConnell Auld adapted a poem by Robert Steel Byrnes which had been written for the opening of the famous John Flynn Memorial Church, Alice Springs, Australia, on 5th

March 1956. Mr. Auld entitled his adaptation 'A Prayer for Kilraughts'

> O Christ Who loves the laden and the lonely,
> And lives among these hills of Carnagee,
> Hear us when from this place now named as holy
> Our praises flow o'er vale and hill to Thee.
>
> Take Thou this house, our planning and our giving,
> And use them, Lord, to Thy strong service brought;
> That men may take the Bread of Life, and living,
> Drink here the cup with love and mercy fraught.
>
> We pray Thee that Thy truth in its uplifting
> May draw men's hearts from sorrow and from pain;
> That in this church the burdened and the drifting
> May touch Thy garment and be whole again.
>
> From these walls tell these ancient hills Thy story
> And breathe it on the good earth and the sand;
> Cause the clear stars to whisper of Thy glory
> And be the living water of this land.
>
> O Living Lord, our strength and consolation,
> In deep compassion bless us when we part;
> Make Thou Thy church the centre of this nation,
> And set Thy Cross within our country's heart.

During the summer of 1975 the church was opened to the public each Sunday afternoon and evening and large numbers came to see it – of all creeds and classes – from all over Northern Ireland.

One of these visitors wrote to the present author:

> "I have just been to see the new First Kilraughts Church and I thought I must write to tell you what a memorable experience it has been.
>
> There is such an air of spaciousness about the whole

70

building and yet the Church itself is so intimate and homely. It has a wonderful atmosphere of worship about it and that is surprising in modern buildings of today. Obviously it has been designed with consummate skill and is a credit to the architect and all the people who were involved.

I loved the antique glass octagons on either side of the entrance door and it was so lovely to see the choir as part of the worshipping congregation and not set apart or sitting looking "face on" at the congregation.

Of course, the magnificent feature is the stained glass windows. The deep hues of the windows behind the pulpit were dramatic but my favourite was the set with Christ in Majesty touching the workaday world of the factory chimneys and the combine harvesters. What a brilliant idea!

First Kilraughts is an inspiring and beautiful church and what a privilege the people have to worship in such a special place Sunday by Sunday."

In addition to the special services, already outlined, Mr. Bell, in the months which followed, invited neighbouring congregations to hold a service in the new church. They came with their minister, choir, organist and people and conducted worship in the evening. A number of congregations accepted the invitation, including Kilraughts Reformed Presbyterian Church. It gave the people a wonderful opportunity to cement friendships and was a happy and uplifting experience for all concerned.

After all of this was over, it could be confidently recorded that the new First Kilraughts Church had been well and truly opened. Now, it was a matter of returning to the challenges of everyday congregational life.

Chapter 2

Notes & References

1. "The Presbyterian Herald", September 1974
2. "The Chronicle" 16th March 1974
3. "The Chronicle", 7th June, 1975
4. Ibid
5. Ibid
6. Ibid
7. Ibid
8. "The Northern Constitution", 14th June 1975
9. Ibid
10. "The Chronicle", 21st June 1975
11. Ibid
12. Ibid
13. "The Chronicle", 5th July 1975
14. Ibid
15. Ibid

Chapter 3

DILIGENCE, DEDICATION and DIGNITY

The Rev. Robert McCausland (Robin) Bell gained great respect and admiration for the way he managed the building of the new church but he never allowed his responsibilities as pastor and preacher to suffer. Indeed it gave him greater enthusiasm and he seemed to throw himself with even more vigour into the everyday life of the congregation.

THE SUNDAY SERVICE

He was seldom out of his pulpit Sunday by Sunday. Determined to be with his people in the difficult period of transition, he was equally committed to his pulpit ministry in the beautiful church he had done so much to create. Each week he preached with passion and dedication and his service followed a fixed order. His first Scripture reading was always from the Old Testament and the second was from the New Testament. In the new church he read these from the lectern and he brought the children to the front for their address. He had much ability to engage with children, for he was a skilled storyteller and they participated with relish. His prayers were carefully structured – the first being a prayer of adoration, thanksgiving and confession and the second of intercession. In it, he tenderly and with carefully chosen words, brought the needs of the world and his own congregation before the Saviour. It was always a wide-ranging prayer and a member, rather irreverently, remarked that if you missed the news bulletins, you could easily catch up on the troubles of the world by listening to Mr. Bell's second prayer! He led the congregation in saying the Lord's Prayer each Sunday and at Communion he led in the repetition of the Creed.

Mr. Bell prefaced each sermon with the announcement of his text and ended with the Ascription of Glory. His sermon notes were on one side of a sheet of paper, but the amount of study

73

involved was evident from the content. The Offering followed the sermon and quite often he came down from the pulpit as the final praise was being sung and pronounced the Benediction from the steps in front of the Communion Table. Then he processed out, down the central aisle and took his position in the vestibule beside the door to the Circular Room. He did not shake hands with the members as they left but was there, available for anyone who wished to speak to him.

For each service he regarded the wearing of robes as "de rigeur" and he took great pains to ensure that all was done with due order and dignity. As one interested in music he took much care about the praise part of the service and tried to ensure that each Sunday psalms, paraphrases and hymns were included. He was pleased with the book of more modern praise items called "Glory to God" and readily embraced these hymns in the Sunday service. However, he was very critical of the way some old hymns had been altered in the new editions of the Church Hymnary. He called it "arrogant desecration" and wrote articles and letters protesting about this. He said the words should remain as the author had written them and no one had any right to interfere with them. They were the authentic creations of these celebrated poets and writers and he could not believe that anyone would be arrogant enough to dare to change them. Whether ancient or modern, each hymn was a product of its time and conveyed its message in its special and individual way and that should be accepted and honoured.

In First Kilraughts, as in most rural congregations, the traditional time for the Sunday service has always been 12 noon. However, in July and August 1987 it was decided that, for those two months only, the service should be held one hour earlier – at 11am. Mr. Bell accepted this as a "useful and helpful experiment"[1] but the Session Minutes show that although "the majority seemed to accept the change, a significant number were unhappy."[2] In 1989 a compromise of 11.30am was agreed for the services in July and August and that has continued ever since.

There were only a few evening services – Pre-Communion and Communion Thanksgiving in May and November, Children's Day, Harvest Thanksgiving and a Christmas Carol Service. Also Kilraughts Young Farmers' Club had an annual evening service each spring. Mr. Bell introduced an evening service on Good Friday. The first took place in "The Stables" in 1972 and in 1994 it was suggested that Communion should be included in this service. However the Kirk Session did not agree and voted 8 to 5 against it.

In 1975 Ballymoney and District Male Voice Choir offered to give a service of sacred music to raise funds for the new church buildings. Mr. Bell was a member of the choir and the senior minister, the Rev. F.A. Robinson, had been its piano accompanist for many years. The service took place on the evening of Sunday, 8th February 1976, and developed into the Annual Praise Service which has become an additional, and much appreciated, evening service each Spring ever since.

A GREAT VISITOR

The Rev. Robin Bell was known far beyond the bounds of his congregation as "a great visitor", and he was worthy of the title, for he gave visitation a high priority in his work.

Depending on the seriousness of the situation, some people were visited once a week, some once a fortnight and he made sure all the elderly and isolated were visited at least once a month. Others, for whom he had a special concern, he visited every three months and every home in the congregation was visited at least once per year. On a number of occasions his visit proved a "life saver", for he found an elderly or isolated member ill or having had an accident in the home. He arrived just in time to summon the aid needed and to give re-assurance and help.

The Rev. Robert McCausland Bell, B.A.
Installed 16th November, 1971
Retired 30th June, 1996
Died 24th October, 2003

In his normal visitation, he never stayed more than half an hour and he always concluded with prayer. Then his exit line was:

"You must excuse me for I have some more doors to knock".

The sympathy and concern which he showed when he visited members in hospital or in residential or nursing homes was also much appreciated. And he not only spoke to the person he had come to visit, but to all around, offering his outstretched hand and comforting word. A Roman Catholic lady in hospital told the present author he prayed by her bedside, at her invitation, every time he visited his own congregational member in her ward. She regarded him as "a good and holy man" whom she held in great respect and esteem.

WEDDINGS AND FUNERALS

He spent many hours preparing for weddings and funerals. He rehearsed each wedding party on an evening before the ceremony with an attention to detail which some of them did not entirely appreciate. He wanted to ensure that everything would be done with order and dignity and everyone would know exactly where to stand, how to move and what to do.

His addresses and prayers at funerals were prepared in depth and with great sensitivity. His committal in the graveyard was often commented on as amongst the most beautiful people had ever heard. He always asked someone to hold his hat during the graveside service and then, when he had concluded the service, he would shake hands with the chief mourners and those standing around, forgetting about the custodian of the hat! This hand shaking could be a lengthy procedure and one, who attended a funeral and was leaving, commented to the man with Mr. Bell's hat that it looked as if he would not get rid of it for a while. The hat-bearer replied:

"I wish he would hurry up, for I am just dying for a smoke!"

If there was a service in the church prior to interment, Mr. Bell always processed in front of the coffin, in his robes, to the graveside.

THE BELL FAMILY HONOURED

Impressed with all the work that he had accomplished and the dedication he and his family had shown, the congregation

*Group at the Presentations to the Bell Family in February, 1980.
Included: Front row (left to right): Mrs. Jane-Anna Connolly, Patricia
and Alexandra Bell, the Rev. Robin and Mrs. Roseanne Bell, Caroline
Bell, the Rev. F.A. Robinson and Mrs. Sarah Brown. Back row:
Mr. and Mrs. W.A. Tweed, Mr. S.A. Blair, Mr. and Mrs. Robert
Patterson. Mr. A. McR. Brown, Mr. and Mrs. James McIlhatton. Mr.
Bell is wearing the robes presented to him and other gifts are
also shown*

felt the need to honour the Rev. Robin Bell, his wife and daughters. This took place twice during his ministry and again at his retirement.

The first time was in February 1980 when, at a largely attended gathering in the Church Hall, Mr. Bell was presented with pulpit robes, a colour television set and a cheque. Mrs. Roseanne Bell was given an electric sewing machine and Patricia, Caroline and Alexandra each received gold necklaces.

Speaking on behalf of the congregation, the present author referred to Mr. Bell's work and said:

> "I do not need to tell anyone in Kilraughts who worked with Mr. Bell during the period of the erection of the Church Building what attention to detail, what care, what steady and constant work, what exertions of energy and what thoughtful planning he put into it all... and what headaches there were also!
>
> This is, in a very real way, his church and we hope he will enjoy being minister of it for many years to come."[3]

After the speeches, Mr. Bell was robed by Mrs. Sarah Brown and Mrs. Jane-Anna Connolly. The television and cheque were presented by the treasurer, Mr. Robert Patterson. Mrs. Charlotte McIlhatton, on behalf of the congregation, presented the electric sewing machine to Mrs. Bell and Mrs. Muriel Tweed presented the jewellery to the Bell girls.

All recipients returned thanks and spoke of their love for Kilraughts. In his speech Mr. Bell said he was particularly pleased to receive new robes and he commented:

> "I will wear these robes with great pride for they are very fine. As I do so, I will ever remember the need to be dressed properly to conduct worship and the fact that much is expected by the Lord of His servant as he goes forth to the pulpit."[4]

In 1991 Mr. Bell celebrated the 30th anniversary of his ordination as a minister of the Presbyterian Church and the 20th anniversary of his installation in First Kilraughts. The congregation marked this milestone with further presentations to Mr. and Mrs. Bell after the morning service on Sunday 3rd March 1991.

The present author spoke of Mr. Bell's coming to First Kilraughts at a very difficult time in the congregation's history

The Rev. Robin and Mrs. Roseanne Bell seated in the two fireside chairs presented to them to celebrate the 30th anniversary of Mr. Bell's ordination and the 20th anniversary of his installation in First Kilraughts. Behind are Mr. Robert Patterson (left) and Mr. S. Alex. Blair. The presentation took place after the morning service on Sunday, 3rd March, 1991

and how he...

> "...gave us the confidence, courage and leadership which eventually produced the fine suite of church buildings we have today."[5]

Mr. Blair also spoke of Mr. Bell's "most conscientious pastoral visitation"[6] and referred to the important place Mrs. Roseanne Bell had in the congregation. He remarked:

> "Her work amongst the girls in the Brownies and Rainbow Guides, her involvement in the PWA and in the Badminton and Bowling Clubs and the interest she

takes in every member of the congregation is something we all greatly value."[7]

Mr. Robert Patterson presented two fireside chairs to Mr. and Mrs. Bell, offering them the thanks and congratulations of the congregation. Both replied saying the chairs were a wonderful gift which would enhance their home and would always remind them of the kindness and generosity they had been shown in First Kilraughts.

PRESENTATIONS

Mr. Bell made a point of making sure that members who had given outstanding service to the church should be thanked and receive gifts of appreciation. A number of such presentations took place during his ministry.

Mr. W. Arthur Tweed was honoured twice for his work as congregational secretary.

When he completed twenty six years in the position he and his wife were made the recipients of gifts at the annual business and social meeting of the congregation on 25th February 1977. The congregation's gift was a suitably inscribed writing desk and a wallet of notes.

Making the presentation, the senior minister, the Rev. F.A. Robinson, recalled his long association with Mr. Tweed and his wife - Arthur and Muriel, as they were known to all. He said Arthur had been a devoted secretary who had the best interests of the congregation at heart. With a smile, Mr. Robinson remarked that sometimes Mr. Tweed held opinions which differed from his but they always amicably agreed to differ and their friendship remained strong and firm. Mrs. Roseanne Bell presented a bouquet to Mrs. Tweed.

In his reply Mr. Tweed spoke of his pride in what he termed, "this fine old congregation of First Kilraughts."[8] He said he had succeeded Mr. Robert Pinkerton, Crosstagherty, as secretary in

*Presentation of a writing desk and wallet of notes to the
congregational secretary, Mr. W. Arthur Tweed, on 25th February,
1977. Included are: The Rev. F.A. Robinson, Mr. Tweed, Mrs.
Roseanne Bell, Mrs. Muriel Tweed and the Rev. Robin Bell*

1950 and only five members of the committee which appointed
him were still alive. He had served five committees and the
members had always treated him with much consideration and
kindness. "Tonight," he said, "is but another indication of that
kindness"[9] and Muriel and he were "most humbled and most
grateful."[10]

When Mr. Tweed retired as secretary a large social gathering
took place in the Church Hall on 9th October 1987 when further
tributes were paid and gifts presented. This time the Rev. Robin
Bell led the congregation's tribute.

Mr. Bell said:

> "The minute books of First Kilraughts are themselves eloquent testimony of the outstanding qualities of Arthur Tweed. His retentive memory and keen brain, his energy and enthusiasm for all aspects of our congregation's life are clearly displayed. His attention to detail, his concern to get to the bottom of anything which he felt required to be examined, his readiness to come to the church at any time when needed, his tireless energy in discharging his duties – all these qualities commended themselves to the Committee which first appointed him and they have served the church well down the years."[11]

Mr. Bell spoke of the demands made on Mr. Tweed when the church was being built. He said:

> "During that time the committee met formally at least twelve times per annum for major business each meeting. Added to that were innumerable sub-committee meetings week after week, month after month. In all this work Arthur never flagged. He was always in good heart and he never failed to give us the benefit of his wisdom and his views."[12]

Mr. Tweed was presented with a silver tea service by Mr. Bell and Mr. Robert Patterson presented him with a cheque on behalf of the congregation. Mrs. Bell presented a bouquet to Mrs. Tweed.

Mr. and Mrs. Tweed were given a standing ovation and in his speech Mr. Tweed recalled many important developments in the congregation during his 37 years as secretary. He said he remembered especially the day he signed, on behalf of First Kilraughts, the contract for the erection of the new church and he commented:

"To commit the congregation to an expenditure of around £150,000 seemed an awful responsibility and one I will never forget."[13]

The senior minister, the Rev. F.A. Robinson, recalled his long association with Mr. Tweed, going back over 60 years. A musical entertainment, a slide show by the present author and supper concluded a memorable night.

The congregational treasurer, Mr. Robert Patterson with his wife, Annie and son, James, were honoured at a gathering in the Church Hall on 30th December 1982.

Presentations to Mr. and Mrs. Robert Patterson and their son James (now Dr. James Patterson) on 30th December, 1982. Included are: Mr. W.A. Tweed, Mr. and Mrs. Patterson and James, Mr. Arnold McClure, the Rev. R. McC. and Mrs. Bell and Mr. Andrew McR. Brown

Paying tribute to Mr. Patterson, the Clerk of Session, Mr. Andrew McR. Brown, said Robert had been a person of diligence and steadfast reliability since his youth. He was an unselfish person, always ready to help. When there were no applications for the position of Church Officer, Mr. Patterson and his wife had voluntarily stepped into the breach and for that the congregation was most grateful.

The Rev. Robin Bell said he was personally indebted to Annie and Robert for many kindnesses shown to him and to his family. Mr. Bell spoke of the esteem in which the Patterson family were held and the gratitude of the congregation for the immense amount of work which they did with no desire for publicity or thanks. He said it would be impossible to list all the things they did week by week which showed their commitment to First Kilraughts. He then presented Mr. Patterson with a wall clock, suitably inscribed, and Mrs. Bell presented Mrs. Patterson with a canteen of cutlery. Their son James, whose birthday it was, and who was home from university, also received a gift. Mr. Arnold McClure, the convener of the Gift Fund, presented Mr. Patterson with a substantial cheque.

In his reply Mr. Patterson said he and his wife had been glad to be of service to the congregation. As treasurer he had always enjoyed the full backing of the committee and people and he concluded:

> "We will cherish these lovely gifts in our home in the years to come and it is our hope that we shall have many years of service yet to offer to our beloved church here in Kilraughts."[14]

At a congregational social in February 1981 Mr. and Mrs. James McIlhatton were honoured for their work with the Freewill Offering. Mr. McIlhatton had been Freewill Offering Secretary for ten years and had been most ably supported by his wife.

The Rev. Robin Bell spoke of their demanding work week by week and thanked them for all they did. He then presented Mr. and Mrs. McIlhatton with an inscribed silver tray and silver condiment set. They both suitably replied, expressing their gratitude for the gifts and their good wishes to the congregation.

When Mr. Andrew McR. Brown, B.Agr., retired from his position as Clerk of Session[15] in 1985 tributes were paid to him in Session and also after the service on Sunday, 2nd March 1986, when presentations were made and a congregational luncheon was given in his honour. The Rev. R. McC Bell spoke of the contribution he and his wife had made to the life of the congregation and he referred especially to Mr. Brown's outstanding work as Clerk of Session for the last twelve years.

Previously the congregation had heard a resolution of appreciation, passed by Kirk Session, which described Mr. Brown as "a most diligent and faithful servant of Jesus Christ". It spoke of his "quiet efficiency, his modest and unassuming manner and his sincere friendliness toward and interest in the members of the congregation."

The resolution continued:

> "A feature of his tenure in office was the dignified way in which he welcomed visiting ministers to our pulpit and his carrying out of his duties at the Communion season. His annual report of Kirk Session to the congregation invariably reflected the individual gifts of mind which were his and provided food for thought for all who heard it."

The resolution concluded:

> "In all his work as Session Clerk, Mr. Brown has been most ably supported by his wife, Mrs. Sarah Brown. To both of them the Kirk Session would pray that they may enjoy many years of peace and continued blessing together."[16]

In a letter of thanks, received in April 1986 Mr. Brown expressed his gratitude for the gifts presented to himself and his wife and commented that the inclement weather experienced during that Spring had given him "ample opportunity to enjoy his very comfortable chair."[17]

A man who showed a special interest in First Kilraughts congregation was Mr. Henry Irwin, Principal of Straidbilly Primary School and Clerk of Session of Bushvale Church. He put his special skills as a photographer and lithographer at the service of First Kilraughts and the congregation's appreciation was shown at a congregational social in February 1978 when Mr. and Mrs. Irwin were honoured.

The Rev. R. McC. Bell said Mr. Irwin had taken many photographs and transparencies of the new church at various stages of its construction and he had also made a detailed photographic account of the opening ceremonies which he presented to the church. As well as that he had inscribed the copy of the book "Kilraughts: A Kirk and Its People" which had been presented to the Moderator on that day. In the new church he had inscribed the lectern Bible, the pulpit Hymn Book and the large photograph of the opening ceremonies which was hung in the vestibule. Mr. Bell said all of this work was much appreciated and added that it was work which was very beautiful, demanded great skill and patience and took up a great deal of Mr. Irwin's time. Mr. Robert Patterson presented Mr. Irwin with a copy of "Kilraughts: A Kirk and Its People" and Mrs. Irwin was the recipient of a bouquet, presented by Mrs. Bell.

Mr. Irwin returned thanks, saying his work had given him great pleasure, for he held Kilraughts Church in very high regard. He also spoke of the excellence of Mr. Blair's book, "Kilraughts: A Kirk and Its People" and added:

> "I will treasure the book for ever, inscribe it appropriately and pass it on to succeeding generations of my family."[18]

VISITORS

In previous generations many Kilraughts people emigrated to places like U.S.A., Canada, Australia and New Zealand and each year Kilraughts has a number of visitors who return to see their Irish cousins and the place where their roots lie. They enjoy worshipping in "the church of their fathers" and all are given a warm welcome. Most go unrecorded but some such visits were especially noteworthy during Mr. Bell's ministry.

On Sunday, 24th June 1984 the Rev. Dr. Bonneau H. Dickson from Atlanta, Georgia, preached in First Kilraughts and he declared:

> "No words can adequately express what it means to me to stand in this pulpit in First Kilraughts Church today. It is the most thrilling moment of my life, for I feel I have really come home."[19]

Dr. Dickson was the descendant of Matthew Dickson who left Artiferral for America and was commended to the Presbyterians there in a letter which he took with him written by his minister, the Rev. Robert Ewing of Kilraughts and dated 12th May 1762.

Dr Bonneau Dickson had been a minister of the American Presbyterian Church for fifty-one years, serving first as a parish minister and later as Executive Secretary of the Atlanta Presbytery. He was visiting his relation, Mr. William Dickson and his family in Ballymoney.

Another visitor who was thrilled to be in First Kilraughts Church was Miss Dorothy Platt from Lakemba, New South Wales, Australia, who attended morning worship on Sunday, 24th June 1990. She later wrote that she found the service emotional and uplifting and was delighted to be in the church of which her great-great grandfather was minister.[20] He was the Rev. Matthew Elder, minister from 1789 to 1827. His son Thomas emigrated to Australia and Miss Platt was his great-granddaughter. Miss Platt, accompanied by the present author, also visited the Rev. Matthew Elder's grave in Kilraughts Old Churchyard.

Four distinguished visitors who came one Sunday morning to see the new church were Sir John and Lady Megaw from Chelsea, London, and the Rt. Rev. Dr. Donald Kennedy, the Bishop of Bombay and Mrs. Kennedy. Sir John and Mrs. Kennedy's father was Mr. Justice R.D. Megaw and their grandfather was Mr. John Megaw, J.P., Ballyboyland (1830-1913).

Mr. Frank May from Adelaide, Australia, visited in 1994 and gave an Evening of Music with local baritone, Mr. William (Billy) Graham. Mr. May was the guest of Kilraughts member, Professor Hugh McGavock, and the evening included five organ solos by Mr. May. Having studied in London at the Royal Academy and the Royal College of Music, Mr. May developed a special interest in the eighteenth century organs of Saxony and frequently came to Europe for study and occasional concerts. First Kilraughts was privileged to have the opportunity to hear Mr. May and the large attendance also enjoyed the singing of Mr. Graham, well-known and much appreciated by all over many years. Mr. Graham contributed six praise items to the memorable evening of praise.

RADIO AND TELEVISION BROADCASTS

Radio and Television also came to Kilraughts on a number of occasions during the ministry of the Rev. Robin Bell.

Part of the Presbytery's Choral Festival from First Kilraughts was broadcast by the BBC as "Sunday Half Hour" on Sunday, 3rd March 1980.

Television cameras came in January 1994 for a "Places Apart" programme for the B.B.C. They televised part of the morning service conducted by Mr. Bell, including the Sacrament of Baptism which was administered during the service. Mr. Bell was interviewed by the presenter, Anne Gregg, famous for her BBC "Holiday" programmes. He explained the stained glass windows and the present author was also interviewed and spoke about the Chi-Rho stone at Drumaquern, which was featured in the programme.

The Chi-Rho stone also featured in a BBC Television "Songs of Praise" from St. James's Presbyterian Church in Ballymoney, transmitted on Sunday, 13th January 1985. Kilraughts Choir took part in the hymn singing, which was conducted by Dr. Havelock Nelson. The organist was Mr. Cecil Thompson and the producer was the Rev. James Skelly. "The Radio Times" gave information about the programme which was broadcast across the United Kingdom. It said:

> "Among those whom Seamus McKee meets is Alex. Blair, a local historian, one of whose main interests is "Old Patrick", an ancient stone that testifies to the district's early links with Christian Europe."[21]

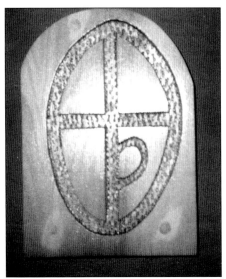

The Chi Rho Stone at Drumaquern was the inspiration for this depiction on the screen of St. Aidan's Church, Didsbury, Manchester. Parishioners saw the stone on the "Songs of Praise" T.V. programme in 1985 and decided to include it in their new screen, which was being designed at the time

90

The parishioners of St. Aidan's Church, Didsbury, Manchester, were installing a new screen in their church. Having seen the television broadcast, they were greatly interested in the Chi Rho Stone and decided to incorporate its design into their screen and this was done in 1986.

The present author also frequently broadcast "Thought for the Day" on Radio Ulster during these years.

SPECIAL SERVICES

Under the auspices of the General Assembly's Public Worship Committee a special Festival of Church Praise was held in First Kilraughts on the evening of Sunday, 31st January 1988. It was aimed at familiarising congregations with "the rich resources to be found in the 3rd edition of the Church Hymnary" and all the congregations of the Presbyteries of Coleraine and Route were invited to be represented. The guest organist was Mr. Adrian Anderson and the guest conductor was Mr. Harold Alexander. Ministers taking part, in addition to Mr. Bell, were the Rev. Dr. A.W.G. Brown, Moderator-designate; the Rev. David Clarke, Moderator of Coleraine Presbytery and the Rev. Sydney McCartney, Moderator of the Route Presbytery. Entitled "Let the People Sing", it was a memorable evening of praise in a church filled to capacity.

The first Sunday in June was traditionally observed, from the time of the Rev. John McCammon, as "the anniversary service" when the foundation of the congregation was celebrated. Mr. Bell continued that tradition and always invited an outstanding minister of the church – often the Moderator – sometimes "outgoing" and sometimes "incoming" for that was also Assembly Week – to be the guest preacher. He also designated that Sunday as "full attendance day" and there was always a large congregation of members together with friends and neighbours.

On Sunday, 19th February 1978 the first "Review" service was held. This was an idea of Mr. Bell to set the various reports of the year's activities within a service of worship. A representative of each of the organisations gave a brief synopsis of that organisation's activities and provision was made for more detailed reports from the Kirk Session and Committee. The minister's remarks put all into context and it proved a very acceptable means of keeping the congregation informed about all that was going on. The service was followed by lunch in the hall, at which the reports were adopted, and this meant there was no need for an annual general meeting, which had been very poorly attended. The "Review" service became an annual feature for the rest of Mr. Bell's ministry in First Kilraughts.

Other changes included taking up an offering at the Communion Service which took place for the first time at the May Communion, 1985. From the beginning of January 1987 it was decided that the announcements should be read at the beginning of the morning service by the Clerk of Session. He was also made responsible for collecting and organizing these announcements.

REPAIRS AT CHURCH AND MANSE

Although the church was a new building there were some matters, mostly of a minor nature, which needed attention. A more major issue was a problem in the roof and the eventual solution to this was to put a new copper roof on the building. This was done in 1982 but a few years later, in May 1986, this roof and the spire were damaged in a dreadful storm which caused much chaos across the North Antrim countryside and repairs were needed. Floodlighting was installed in 1988.

The Manse had undergone some repairs for the arrival of the Bell family and in September 1987 a new kitchen was installed. In 1993 it was discovered that a very serious problem of dry rot had been detected in the woodwork of six rooms at the Manse, three on each floor at the front of the house. This had to be attended to urgently and on 15th September 1993 a major scheme of refurbishment and widescale repairs was begun, Mr. J.S. Dunlop's firm being engaged to undertake the work. A Buildings' Sub-Committee consisting of Mr. Bell, Mr. Robert Patterson, Mr. Bob Richmond and Mr. James McIlhatton was appointed and members of committee undertook a visitation of the congregation in November 1993 to obtain funds for the project.

Later the committee was informed that the older section, at the rear of the Manse, was also affected but the need to deal with it was judged by the experts to be less urgent. It was therefore decided to proceed with the front six rooms and leave the second phase until later. Work went on apace and was completed early in 1994. It was thought that the Bell family would have to vacate the premises for a time but they decided to stay. For a number of months they tolerated very restricted and difficult living conditions but, despite all the chaos, dust and upheaval, they never complained, accepting it all and coping as best they could. The congregation responded generously to the appeal for funds and promised around thirteen and a half thousand pounds on an annual basis until the debt would be cleared. There was also an anonymous donation of five thousand pounds to the Building Fund. The façade of the Manse was rebuilt and, with new floors and re-decoration, there were many favourable comments on what a good job had been done. The Committee and members visited and were impressed.

VISITATION OF PRESBYTERY, APRIL, 1989

The Route Presbytery held a Visitation at First Kilraughts on 4th and 17th April 1989 and their "Finding" spoke of Mr. Bell's "diligence" and said:

> "First Kilraughts continues its fine historic witness as a steady and solid congregation.....We are grateful for the ongoing witness of First Kilraughts and for the encouragement the people give to the Presbytery in the

fellowship of the Gospel. Each member can be proud of the congregation's history, privileged to belong to the church in the present and challenged to share the responsibility of making the fellowship even stronger in the future".[22]

One hundred and eighty-eight had been returned as the number of families and Presbytery noted that this showed "no significant change" on eight years ago. Average attendance at morning worship was recorded as 205 and the sacraments of Baptism and the Lord's Supper were "regularly and conscientiously observed". Presbytery noted that there was a Morning Sunday School and Bible Class in the church and an afternoon school at Craigatempin. There was also a Children's Church and Presbytery felt the crèche might be re-started. They detected a "buoyancy" about the Youth organisations which were listed as Boys' Brigade, Brownies, Junior Badminton and Youth Fellowship.

The Finding commended the work of the ladies in the P.W.A. and commented:

> "Perhaps their contribution will be recognised by the election of women to the Kirk Session and Congregational Committee".[23]

The Finding quoted the words of the Clerk of Session, the present author, who had said:

> "The congregation endeavours to witness in our local area but is also mindful of the needs of others, especially in a year like this when disaster and tragedy seem to follow one another in various parts of the world. We offer our money and our prayers wherever there is need and we enrich ourselves in so doing."[24]

Commending these words to all, the Finding concluded:

> "That sums up the tone and spirit of this congregation and is a most laudable objective to have in view."[25]

GIFT

Miss Eileen Mathews, formerly of Kilmandil, was most generous to the congregation of her birth. As we have already seen she gave a number of valuable gifts to the new church and in 1984 she presented Bibles for the pews.

THE STABLES

Most churches in the nineteenth and early twentieth centuries had long rows of stables to accommodate the horses which brought the people to church. At one stage First Kilraughts had over sixty stalls available, but in December 1932, with the advent of the bicycle and the motor car, it was decided to demolish the "lower stables" along the top of the graveyard. The "upper stables" with twenty-six stalls remained and were in use up to

The Rev. R. McC. Bell re-opens "The Stables" as clubrooms for Kilraughts Y.F.C. after extensive repairs, 1st September, 1990. Looking on are (left to right): Mrs. Pam Robinson, Y.F.C.U. Secretary; Messrs. D.J. Dunlop, Club President; S.A. Blair; Wm. Christie, contractor, and Andrew McNeill, Club Leader; Miss Donna McFadden, Secretary and the Y.F.C.U. President, Mr. Tom Topping. The Stables were a great asset to the congregation in the period between the fire and the opening of the new Church

the Second World War. In 1967 a part of these was converted into clubrooms for Kilraughts Young Farmers and were officially opened by the minister of First Kilraughts, the Rev. F.A. Robinson, on 19th September 1970. This accommodation proved invaluable to the church during the period after the fire, but by the 1980's the stables began to suffer from damp and were in need of repair. It was decided that a wide-scale refurbishment programme would have to be carried out. This involved the provision of a new roof and the installation of a new fitted kitchen.

The Rev. Robin Bell was given the honour of re-opening the building on 1st September 1990. The managing-director of Christie Developments, Mr. William Christie, who had been responsible for the work, presented him with a commemorative key and Mr. Bell performed the re-opening ceremony. As he did so, he paid tribute to the excellence of the work which had been carried out and thanked Kilraughts Y.F.C. for all their co-operation and help when the church depended on them for accommodation for many activities and events. He said the congregation owed the Y.F.C. a very big debt of gratitude for all they had done.

RELATIONS WITH NEIGHBOURING CHURCHES

The Rev. Robin Bell was always happy to foster friendship and good relationships with the other local Presbyterian churches and with churches of other denominations in the area.

There was a close relationship with the neighbouring Presbyterian churches of Bushvale, Roseyards and Ballyweaney. When the minister of Roseyards, the Rev. W.J. Watson was honoured with an M.B.E. by H.M. the Queen in the New Year's Honours List of 1996 he received the congratulations of First Kilraughts.

In his reply to the good wishes, Mr. Watson wrote:

"My early association with First Kilraughts was through my friendship with the late Rev. F.A. and Mrs. Robinson, both of whom I met and with whom I spent the afternoon of the day I preached "on trial" for Roseyards forty years ago."[26]

The letter was to the present author and Mr. Watson continued:

"Then there has been my happy association with First Kilraughts congregation through the membership and fellowship of Kilraughts Y.F.C. for whose members I have had such a great admiration and affection, as I have also for yourself."[27]

Speaking of Mr. Bell, he wrote:

"My friendship with your minister, the Rev. Robin Bell, has been long standing. We attended the same school – Regent House – and then he and my younger brother, John, were together assistant ministers to the Rev. J.B. McIlroy in McQuiston Memorial Church in Belfast."[28]

Mr. Watson concluded:

"So, it is no wonder that I have so many happy memories of my association with First Kilraughts. Please convey to the minister and Kirk Session my very deep appreciation of their kindness and thoughtfulness.

Sincerely,

W.J."[29]

For many years the church of Ireland had a small mission station along the Loughabbin Road but this had closed before Mr. Bell came to Kilraughts. However he maintained a warm friendship with the two neighbouring Church of Ireland parishes of Ballymoney and Loughgiel.

For over a century and more there has been a special friendship between First Kilraughts and Kilraughts Reformed Presbyterian Church. This happy relationship of mutual co-operation and esteem was continued by Mr. Bell and the minister of Kilraughts R.P. Church, the Rev. Professor Frederick S. Leahy.

When the Synod of the R.P. Church came to Kilraughts in June 1981 the Women's Missionary Rally took place in First Kilraughts church and the ladies of the congregation provided a meal for all the Synod delegates in First Kilraughts Church Hall.

On 28th May 1983 when Kilraughts R.P. church celebrated the bicentenary of its foundation with an open air service at Kirkhills, Mr. Bell took part in the service. In Kilraughts R.P. church afterwards he and the present author brought the greetings and good wishes of the people of First Kilraughts to the Covenanters on that important milestone in their history.

Professor Leahy retired in 1988 and a letter of good wishes was sent to him from First Kilraughts

In his reply Professor Leahy spoke of the good relations between the two congregations and expressed the hope that "such a spirit of goodwill may long continue."[30] His successor, the Rev. Harry Coulter, continued this and was one of the speakers at Mr. Bell's retirement gathering.

First of the local clergy to offer the hand of friendship to Mr. Bell on arrival in First Kilraughts was the Parish Priest of Loughgiel, the Very Rev. Canon George Clenaghan. He gave a high priority to maintaining good relations with his Protestant neighbours and attended functions in First Kilraughts from time to time. Mr. Bell and the present author represented First Kilraughts congregation at Canon Clenaghan's funeral in St. Patrick's Church, Loughgiel in September 1981.

The Rev. John Barrett, P.P. (1979-1985) continued the good

relations which Canon Clenaghan had built up. The work was carried on with enthusiasm by the next Parish Priest, the Very Rev. Canon Kevin Donnelly, whose cheerful personality and great gift for friendship have made him a person held in high esteem by the whole North Antrim community. He was anxious to have close relationships between his people and the people of Kilraughts and in 1994 wrote to Mr. Bell suggesting one way of cementing friendship would be for the organisations to meet and he suggested that the Bowling Clubs and the Badminton Clubs of the two churches might come together for friendly matches. Kirk Session gave this their blessing saying it was

> "…a positive contribution to the building up of the friendship and harmony which both churches desire."[31]

BEYOND KILRAUGHTS

Mr. Bell was involved in much work in the wider church at Presbytery and Assembly level and also in inter-church relations.

He was Moderator of the Route Presbytery in 1981 and for many years was the Presbytery's convener of the Committee on Church Property and convener of the World Development Appeal. At Assembly level he served on the Inter-Church Relations Board and the Board of Finance and Administration.

The many debates about membership of the World Council of Churches and the Presbyterian Church's withdrawal in 1980 troubled Mr. Bell considerably. He was very aware that such debates and disagreements did not make for a peaceful or united church and this grieved him. He was also perturbed about the debates on ecumenism and the anti-ecumenist stance of many which dominated Assembly meetings through the 1970's and 1980's. He was committed to dialogue with all denominations for he believed only by doing this could understanding and respect for each others' position be achieved. He gave much energy and time to the "Friends of the Way", of which he was secretary. This group of ministers and priests met monthly for Bible Study and fellowship. He was very proud of the friendship and understanding which came about as a result of these contacts.

THE TROUBLES

The whole of Mr. Bell's ministry in First Kilraughts took place against the background of "The Troubles". It was a dark period in the history of our province with terror, distress, destruction and death a daily occurrence.

Soon after he arrived, there were "Prayers for Peace" at Ballymoney Diamond on the afternoon of Sunday, 1st October 1972 and he and the present author took part with local ministers, priests and lay people. It was estimated that over two thousand people were present for the event.

In 1973 the idea of a devolved power-sharing executive was discussed and Mr. Bell reported on this to the Route Presbytery, commenting also on the continuing violence, intimidation and political and religious discrimination evident in many places.

In 1974 signatures for a Witness for Peace were taken and most of First Kilraughts congregation signed.

1981 was an especially bleak year with the IRA hunger strikes raising tension considerably. The tension became worse when the South Belfast Unionist MP, the Rev. Robert Bradford, was murdered by the IRA. In an attempt to calm a volatile situation, periods of silence and prayer were held in many towns. In Ballymoney a large crowd assembled and a number of local ministers participated. However, when the parish priest, the Very Rev. Daniel McBride appeared, he was greeted by "boohs" from a section of the crowd. When Mr. Bell saw what was happening, he left the platform and went to Father McBride, shaking him by the hand and conveying him to the platform to stand with the other clergy there. This was greeted with loud cheering. It was a courageous act in the tension of the time and showed the calibre of Mr. Bell.

The signing of the Anglo-Irish Agreement on 15th November 1985 caused much consternation and again Presbytery called on Mr. Bell to formulate a resolution expressing concern but at the same time calling on the people to remain calm and comply with the Moderator's call for prayer.

One of the most horrific events of "The Troubles" in North Antrim was the burning to death of the Quinn children in their home on the Carnany Estate in Ballymoney in the early hours of the twelfth of July 1998. Kilraughts, like many places far and near, was shocked and Mr. Bell and the present author attended the children's funeral in the Church of Our Lady and St. Patrick, Ballymoney, amidst unprecedented scenes of anguish and distress and with the world's media looking on.

MURDER OF RESERVE CONSTABLE JOHN W. MOORE

Kilraughts did not completely escape "The Troubles" for, on the morning of Saturday, 15th April 1978, a member of the congregation, Reserve Constable John Wilson Moore, was murdered in the laneway of his farm at Ballycraigagh.

He was going out to attend to his flock of sheep when his car came into contact with a fishing line which had been stretched across the lane. This set off the booby-trap bomb which killed Mr. Moore and also killed his dog, which was beside him in the car and a lamb which had been unwell and which he had brought in for some special attention.

Well-known in the community, Mr Moore was a life-long member of First Kilraughts Church, secretary of Moyarget Masonic Lodge, a member of Ballycastle Royal Arch Chapter of Masons, and enjoyed playing bowls as a member of Bushvale Bowling Club. His murder made headlines in press, radio and television and was widely condemned. Speaking at Mass in

Magherahoney Roman Catholic Church, the Rev. Father John Barrett condemned the killing of what he termed "a harmless man" and appealed to the IRA to end "their inhuman slaughter and allow ordinary people to live peacefully."[32] Similar condemnation was voiced by the Parish Priest of Loughgiel, the Very Rev. Canon George Clenaghan, and in all the local Protestant churches reference was made to the tragedy and sympathy expressed to Mr. Moore's family circle.

The North Antrim Unionist Association issued a statement saying:

> "We demand the Secretary of State to introduce forthwith the necessary measures to expedite the removal from society of the perpetrators of such dastardly crimes. Present policies to deal with terrorists are totally inadequate and only encourage, in the present tit-for-tat situation which exists in the Province, further bloodshed and unnecessary loss of life."[33]

At a meeting of Ballymoney Borough Council on Monday, 17th April, the Mayor, Councillor Mrs. M. J. Holmes, O.B.E., J.P., said she knew Constable Moore personally and was shattered to think that...

> "in this community there are those who are prepared to perpetrate such dreadful acts."[34]

Councillor Hugo Boyle, who also knew Constable Moore, said he was...

> "a big quiet fellow and one of nature's gentlemen."[35]

The Council members stood in silence as a mark of respect and, led by the Mayor, many of them attended the funeral, which took place in First Kilraughts Church the next day, Tuesday, 18th April 1978. The church buildings could not hold all who were present and when the vestibule and ancillary rooms were filled, hundreds had to stand outside.

The service was conducted by the minister, the Rev. R. McC. Bell, who said the attack on Constable Moore had been "most calculated and cowardly."[30] Mr. Bell told the huge gathering that a year ago an attempt had been made on Mr. Moore's life and all who knew him as a friend were relieved that, on that occasion, he was physically unharmed. It was typical of his courage that, as soon as the disturbance was over, he returned to his life of service to the community both as a farmer and as a member of the RUC Reserve. His aim was to do what he could to help his country in the struggle against lawlessness and it would be difficult to find a friendlier, more peace-loving man than John Moore.

Mr. Bell went on:

> "Members of our Security Forces, full-time and part-time alike, together with their families, and many other citizens from all shades of society are being subjected to vicious attacks at all hours of the day and night. No political goal can justify these appalling crimes.
>
> To appeal to the ringleaders to call off their murder-gangs is a futile exercise as such appeals are neither heeded nor heard. A woman who will wheel a bomb concealed by a baby into the centre of a town is not reached by mere appeal. A man who will lay a wire across a lane in the hours of darkness is not going to stop doing it because the community asks him to stop. The people to whom we appeal to-day are the folk who are sheltering these murderers in the so- called "safe" houses. They must realise that they are guilty every bit as much as the people who mined the lane and who carried the guns. To them I say: 'Keep your doors closed against those who will use your house to promote death and violence. Give the authorities the information they require to enable them to bring these criminals to justice.'

To Mr. Moore's sister and his family circle we express our deep sympathy in their great loss.

In paying our tribute to the life of our friend, some words of the Apostle Paul would seem appropriate. 'For we who live are always delivered unto death for Jesus' sake, that the life also of Jesus might be made manifest in our mortal flesh.' John Wilson Moore has joined the ranks of those who gave their all for God and their country. He will be remembered in this church and district as a true Christian soldier, who followed his Great Captain and Leader to the end."[37]

The senior minister, the Rev. F.A. Robinson, and the Moderator of the Route Presbytery, the Rev. John Hume, Dunluce, took part in the service. The Moderator of the General Assembly, the Rt. Rev. Dr. Tom Patterson, led prayers and in a short address said:

"We are reminded here to-day of the great debt we owe to the security forces. When a man gives his life, he gives everything. And John Wilson Moore gave his life. To-day we give thanks to God for the sacrifice of so many members of the security forces these past years. This is the latest part of a long story of devotion to duty and great sacrifice both in the giving of life and giving up of so many things that we cannot begin to appreciate."[38]

The R.U.C. Band played and R.U.C. colleagues were pall-bearers as the cortege made its way from the church to the graveyard. At the graveside there was a scripture reading by the Rev. John A. Patton, Bushvale, and Mr. Bell conducted the committal.

Mr. Moore was survived by his sister, Mrs. Nellie Sterrett, Exeter, and a wide circle of friends. He had been a member of the RUC Reserve from its inception and had only six months to serve before he would have reached the retirement age of 60 years.

Many representatives of the public life of Northern Ireland attended the funeral including the local M.P. the Rev. Dr Ian Paisley, and dignitaries representing the Secretary of State, the GOC, the Police Authority and the Ulster Defence Regiment. The R.U.C. delegation was led by the Deputy Chief Constable Jack Hermon and also in the congregation were the Very Rev. Canon George Clenaghan, P.P. Loughgiel, and the Rev. John Barrett, C.C., Magherahoney.

Many commented on the solemnity of the occasion, the dignity with which everything had been carried out, the beauty of the church building and the excellence of Mr. Bell's address. The funeral was given coverage by the media across the United Kingdom and Mr. Bell's words were quoted on radio and television, as well as in the press both locally and nationally.

MEMORIALS TO JOHN W. MOORE

On the evening of Sunday, 22nd April 1979, at a special service in First Kilraughts, memorial gifts were dedicated to commemorate Reserve Constable John W. Moore.

Mr. Moore's colleagues in the Royal Ulster Constabulary and the R.U.C. Reserve presented a brass tablet, placed in the vestibule, bearing the crest of the R.U.C. and inscribed:

"To the Glory of God
and
In Honoured Memory of
Reserve Constable John Wilson Moore
Royal Ulster Constabulary
who gave his life in the execution of his duty
15th April 1978
"Greater Love Hath No Man Than This""

The formal presentation of the tablet was made by the Chief Constable of the R.U.C., Sir Kenneth Newman, and it was unveiled by Mr. Moore's cousin, Mrs. Violet Gillan.

Unveiling the Memorial Tablet to Reserve Constable John W. Moore, R.U.C., 22nd April 1979. Left to right: Messrs. Tom Henry and Walter McBride, neighbours of Mr. Moore; the Rt. Rev. Dr. David Burke, Moderator of the General Assembly, who dedicated the memorial; Mrs. Violet Gillan, Mr. Moore's cousin who unveiled the Memorial Tablet; Sir Kenneth Newman, Chief Constible of the R.U.C.; Lady Newman; the Rev. R. McC. Bell and Mr. J. Gillan

First Kilraughts congregation's memorial of thirty trees and shrubs of different varieties, planted in the grounds of the church, was formally presented by the minister of First Kilraughts, the Rev. R. McC. Bell, and both gifts were dedicated by the Moderator of the General Assembly, the Rt. Rev. Dr. David Burke. The congregation used the rest of the money, which had been subscribed, to set up a John Moore Memorial Fund to help finance the work of Christian Education among the young people of First Kilraughts. This included special John Moore Memorial prizes awarded for creative efforts by the pupils of the Morning Sunday School.

Ministers who took part in the service which followed the unveiling of the Memorial Tablet to Reserve Constable John W. Moore, 22nd April 1979, photographed with the Chief Constable, Sir Kenneth Newman.
Left to right; The Rev. H. L. Henry, Moderator of Synod; the Rt. Rev.
Dr. David Burke, Moderator of the General Assembly; the Rev. R. McC.
Bell; the Rev. J.G. Leitch, Clerk of Presbytery and the Rev. W.J. Watson,
Moderator of Presbytery

In an appreciation of Reserve Constable Moore, the Rev. R. McC. Bell said that the uppermost thought in the minds of those who knew him was of Mr. Moore's quiet friendliness. He said:

> "In church and community life, on his farm at Ballycraigagh, in the homes of neighbours and friends, where he was always a welcome visitor, and in the course of his security duty in uniform, he was always the same – quiet, helpful, ready to serve, willing to do any helpful act that was asked of him, and many more which originated in his own generous and unselfish heart.

He saw his work in the Police Reserve as a service which he felt called upon to perform for his country and community. He found much fulfilment and satisfaction, comradeship and fellowship in the Reserve, and the main source of this was the knowledge that he was helping others along the road to peace.

John Moore loved God, and was a faithful member of this church. He attended services very regularly, and he gladly gave his support to its funds, both in his lifetime and by a most generous bequest after his death.

He was a man of the country. He loved the good earth, and he had a great interest in things that grew. Thus when the question of a permanent memorial to him was

Police colleagues of Reserve Constable John W. Moore pay their tribute to his memory at the Memorial Tablet

discussed, and when we knew that a very magnificent tablet in brass was to be presented by his friends in the Police Service, it was felt that a plantation of trees would be a memorial in the grounds of the church that would have given him much pleasure. Thus the thirty newly planted trees of differing varieties are to be his memorial. His name will also be permanently linked with the Christian Education of our young people and in future there will be a memorial prize each year to be presented in his name.

John Moore is greatly missed in the congregation which he loved, in the fellowship of the Indoor Bowling Club at Bushvale where he had many friends, in the Masonic fraternity at Moyarget and Ballycastle where he was held in high regard, in the ranks of his Royal Ulster Constabulary Reserve colleagues with whom he served and most of all, among the good folk of Ballycraigagh and Culbane, who knew him as friend and neighbour over many years."[39]

Mr. Bell concluded his tribute with these words:

"We today salute his courage and his unfaltering devotion to duty. He would have been the last person on earth to think of himself in heroic terms yet that is in fact what he is. Knowing full well the dangers of the work which he had undertaken, he was undaunted by them and he went forward to the task with cheerful Christian fortitude and faith. By his great self-sacrifice he has shown that he believed in the ultimate triumph of good over evil, and he has entered into the reality of an imperishable hope."[40]

The service began with the call to worship and prayer of invocation by the Rev. W.J. Watson, Moderator of the Route Presbytery, and the Rev. H. Laurence Henry, Moderator of the Synod of Ballymena and Coleraine, led in the prayers of confession and petition. The prayer of intercession was taken by the Rev. J.G. Leitch, Clerk of the Route Presbytery. Scripture lessons were read by Chief Inspector J. N. Howe, R.U.C., and Reserve Constable R.B. Bodkin, R.U.C. The augmented church choir sang the anthem, "How Great Thou Art," and Mr. Howard Gillespie was the organist.

The Moderator of the General Assembly, the Rt. Rev. Dr. David Burke preached the sermon taking as his text the words from the 18th chapter of the Book of Genesis: "Shall not the Judge of all the earth do right?" He paid tribute to the courage and steadfastness of the R.U.C. in the fight against terrorism and spoke of the dilemmas facing the Christian in Ulster's strife-torn society. The Moderator said it was necessary for the Church to spell out in practical terms the interpretation of justice for all in the context of Christian love. "Mr. Callaghan", he said, "had spoken this week of the 99.9 per cent in the Province who were not involved in the violence. Surely the main function of the State is to protect that 99.9 per cent." Dr. Burke reiterated that no political expediency or fear of the electorate should be allowed to hinder the forces of law and order or prevent evil-doers from being brought to justice.

The Moderator concluded by referring to the moral dilemmas which faced the police. He said:

> "They have a moral responsibility to prevent further heartbreak and desolation in the families of the community and yet are under constant criticism concerning alleged methods used to get information for successful prosecution."[41]

Mr. Bell welcomed the large congregation which packed the church and overflowed into the vestibule. Among those present, as well as the Chief Constable and Lady Newman, were Deputy Chief Constable D.H. Johnston and Mrs. Johnston; Mr. William

Taylor, Secretary of the Policy Authority and Mrs. Taylor, and a number of Senior Officers of the R.U.C. as well as a large number of men and women from the ranks of the R.U.C. and the R.U.C.R.

Mrs. Eileen Paisley represented her husband, the Rev. Dr. Ian Paisley, M.P. and the Aldermen and Councillors of Ballymoney Borough Council were led by the Mayor, Councillor Mrs. Mollie Holmes; the Deputy Mayor, Councillor Robert McComb and the Clerk, Mr. W. J. Williamson. Brigadier C.I. Shortts of the 8th Infantry Brigade, represented the Army and Major K. Alexander represented the U.D.R. There were also personnel from the Army, U.D.R. and Auxiliary Services in the congregation, a number of local clergy and the Kirk Session of First Kilraughts Church.

An apology was received from the Secretary of State for Northern Ireland, Mr. Roy Mason and Mrs. Mason. Mr. Mason had hoped to be present but had to return to London on urgent business.

The ladies of First Kilraughts served supper to all in the Church Hall and thanks to them were expressed by Chief Inspector J.N. Howe, R.U.C., and the Moderator, Dr. Burke. In October 1986 the congregation agreed, with the assent of Mrs. Gillan, Mr. Moore's cousin, to accept custody of the Police Medal which had been posthumously awarded to Constable Moore. The presentation was made by a delegation from Ballymoney R.U.C. led by Chief Inspector Joshua Chambers and Sergeant John Long. So the church has in its keeping a number of memorials to the only member of the congregation to be killed in "The Troubles".

TRAGEDY AT "CHURCH VIEW"

> "We meet under the shadow of a great tragedy. At our neighbouring farm of "Church View" a tragedy

unfolded last night of death and horror which our countryside has never known before."[42]

That was how the present author addressed a stunned congregation at the morning service on Sunday, 10th September 1995. In the absence of the minister, he was speaking of the deaths of three young men at the home of the McClure family, whose farm is just opposite the church building.

A young plumber, Derek Cushnahan, had been working in a thirty foot well in the farm yard when he collapsed. The Fire Service came and a fireman, Robin Neill, went into the well to rescue Mr. Cushnahan. He died, as did a member of the paramedic ambulance team, Allister Barr, who made a further rescue bid. Later Mr. Cushnahan died also so that three young lives were lost.

Mr. Blair spoke of the "unselfish and heroic courage" of Mr. Neill and Mr. Barr and of Mr. Cushnahan's "gesture of neighbourliness and kindness" which had developed into such a dreadful tragedy. He also spoke of the McClure family, "esteemed members of our congregation, so suddenly caught up in such horrific events."[43]

The Rev. Robin Bell attended the funerals of the men and also offered the congregation's sympathy to all involved. Mr. Neill's sister is a member of First Kilraughts – Mrs. Margaret Brown, Gorsebank.

RETIREMENT

It was announced on 1st October 1995 that Mrs. Roseanne Bell had retired as leader of the Brownies and Rainbow Guides in the congregation. At a specially called meeting of Kirk Session, held on Monday 12th February 1996, Mr. Bell informed the elders of his intention to retire from the active ministry on 30th June 1996. He said:

"By early summer I shall have completed thirty-five

The Rev. Robin and Mrs. Roseanne Bell, at the time of Mr. Bell's retirement

years service since ordination and a total of forty years full-time ministerial involvement in the Presbyterian Church in Ireland since my date of licensure, 25th May 1956."[44]

He knew he could remain for five more years, until he was seventy years of age and, he continued:

> "There would be several strong reasons for taking advantage of this allowance – chiefly the feeling of being part of a warm-hearted, friendly congregation from which I receive great encouragement and work satisfaction. Also there is the constant thrill of conducting worship in our superbly beautiful church building and I have a great reluctance to take a step which would bring that situation to an end."[45]

However, he said there were many challenges ahead and he

believed a new minister would have the enthusiasm to meet these challenges. He felt it was time for him to step aside.

The present author said Mr. Bell would be hard to replace and all were sad to hear his decision. However they would have no desire to deny him the enjoyment of what they hoped would be for him and for Mrs. Bell a long and happy retirement.

Mr. Blair added:

> "We go forward to the future, the better equipped for it by your ministry and all your work among us."[46]

PRESENTATIONS

Many organizations presented gifts to Mr. and Mrs. Bell before they left First Kilraughts. These included P.W.A., the Choir, the Bible Study Group, Morning Sunday School, Craigatempin Afternoon Sunday School, the Indoor Bowling Club, the Youth Fellowship, the Girls' Fellowship, the Junior and Senior Badminton Clubs, the Second Route Company of the Boys' Brigade and Kilraughts Brownies and Rainbow Guides. All of these gifts Mr. and Mrs. Bell described as "most humbling and incredibly generous". At an informal meeting of Kirk Session on 2nd June 1996 Mr. Bell presented each member with a Presbyterian tie as his personal gift of appreciation to them. Mr. and Mrs. Bell also presented a table cloth for the Communion table before they left.

The Rev. Robin Bell preached his farewell sermon on Sunday 30th June 1996 and, with his wife, greeted each member at the close of the service. Presbytery appointed the Rev. J. Trevor Magowan, B.A., B.D., minister of St. James's church, Ballymoney, as convener-in-charge of the congregation and interim-Moderator of Session from 1st July 1996.

The main congregational farewell and presentation of gifts took place at a great gathering in the Robinson Hall on the evening of Friday, 26th July 1996. The attendance included family and friends of Mr. and Mrs. Bell, many ministerial colleagues from the Presbyterian Church, the Rev. Harry Coulter, Kilraughts R.P. Church and the Very Rev. Canon Kevin Donnelly, P.P. Loughgiel.

Mr. and Mrs. Bell had moved to a new home at Knockhill Park in Ballymoney which they called "Glen Orchy" after one of their favourite places in Scotland, but it was obvious they were missing Kilraughts. Mr. Bell began his speech:

> "My first word this evening must be an expression of the very great joy that it gives to Roseanne and me to be in Kilraughts. We have missed you all greatly and are delighted to be back amongst our own Kilraughts people tonight."[47]

He spoke about his time as minister in Kilraughts, the joy he had had in planning the new church and the many people in the congregation who had given outstanding service.

In his tribute to Mr. Bell, the present author mentioned that Mr. Bell had always been busy. There was, he said:

> "....a congregation to look after, organizations to support, events to plan, people to visit and a community to serve."[48]

Mr. Bell had given himself fully in the service of the congregation and was known throughout the whole countryside as "a great visitor."

Taking this up, in his speech, Mr. Bell said what a privilege it was to be made welcome in people's homes. He continued:

> "Home is the place where people really are their true selves and a minister cannot serve God effectively if he or she does not build a strong link with the home life of each family."[49]

The present which Mr. Bell had modestly requested, when

*Group at the Retirement Presentations to the Rev. Robin and Mrs. Roseanne
Bell, 26th July, 1996. Front row (left to right): Mr. A. McR. Brown, the Rev.
Robin Bell and Mr. Robert Patterson. At the back are Mr. S. Alex. Blair and
Mrs. Roseanne Bell*

asked what he would like as a retirement gift, was a composite
picture of the three sets of stained glass windows in the church.
This he was given, the presentation being made by Mr. Andrew
McR. Brown, but he was also given a substantial cheque from
the congregation, this presentation being made by the church
treasurer, Mr. Robert Patterson.

Miss Lilian Elliott, on behalf of the congregation, presented
Mrs. Bell with a gold chain and an inscribed Bible. Miss Elliott
also presented gifts to Mr. and Mrs. Bell's three daughters – Miss
Patricia Bell, Mrs. Caroline Havard and Miss Alexandra Bell.

116

The oldest girl in the Brownie Pack, Alison Murray, and the youngest, Kathryn Watt, presented flowers to Mrs. Bell, who founded the Brownies and Rainbow Guides in First Kilraughts.

In her speech of thanks, Mrs. Roseanne Bell said how much she would treasure the gifts and how hard it was to leave Kilraughts but she concluded:

> "We will continue to feel part of you and remember you often, asking for God's blessing on you in the months and years ahead."[50]

Speaking on behalf of her sisters, Miss Patricia Bell said it was so nice to be remembered by the congregation and spoke of the affection they all had for First Kilraughts and for the Manse in which they had grown up.

The Very Rev. Dr. A.W. Godfrey Brown, Ballycastle, Moderator of the Route Presbytery, Moderator of the Synod of Ballymena and Coleraine, and former Moderator of the General Assembly, brought the greetings, congratulations and good wishes of these three bodies to Mr. and Mrs. Bell and the congregation on what he said was "an outstanding and memorable occasion."[51]

Supper was served and a concert programme followed. Those taking part included the Church Choir and Trio (Grace Lamont, Charlotte McIlhatton and Janette Reid), the Young Musicians Group, the Dunloy Accordian Orchestra, Jack Wilkinson (bass) and William Graham (tenor). Two of Mr. and Mrs. Bell's daughters, Alexandra and Caroline, sang solos and Mrs. Betty Robinson read a poem she had specially written for the occasion. The church organist, Mr. Maurice Christie, was accompanist, and a vote of thanks was proposed by Mr. Bell's brother, Mr. Barry Bell, Belfast. The evening concluded – and by that time it was almost midnight – with the singing of Psalm 23 and the Benediction pronounced by Mr. Bell.

It was the end of an era in First Kilraughts but the present author commented that night that Mr. Bell had left Kilraughts "a harmonious and happy congregation". He said:

> "We are full of vitality and strength, we have a beautiful church building, organisations enthusiastic and ever moving forward and a community enriched by our church's presence and especially by the ministry of the Rev. Robin Bell."[52]

Retirement brought much happiness for Mr. and Mrs. Bell. Unfortunately it was all too brief. Although Mrs. Bell was able to look after her husband in his final months, she had been diagnosed with a serious illness. The Rev. Robin Bell died on 24th October 2003 aged 72 years. He was cremated and a private funeral service was held at Roselawn, Belfast, conducted by his close friend, the Very Rev. Professor Finlay Holmes. On that same afternoon of Wednesday, 29th October 2003 a service of thanksgiving for his life and work was held in First Kilraughts. The Rev. Noel McClean, the present minister, conducted the service and the address was given by the Rev. Kenneth D.W. Crowe, minister of Bushvale, the church which Mr. and Mrs. Bell attended during their retirement. Ballymoney Male Voice Choir sang and prayers were offered by the Moderator of the General Assembly, the Rt. Rev. Dr. Ian A. McKay. The congregational praise included a favourite psalm, paraphrase and hymn of Mr. Bell – Psalm 121: "I to the hills will lift mine eyes"; paraphrase 61: "Bless'd be the everlasting God, the Father of our Lord" and the hymn "Love Divine". Mr. Bell's ashes were interred in First Kilraughts churchyard.

MEMORIAL MINUTE

Later the Kirk Session passed the following Memorial Minute:

> "It is with deep regret that the Kirk Session records the death, which took place on Friday 24th October

2003, of their beloved Senior Minister, the Rev. Robert McCausland Bell. He was in the 73rd year of his age and the 43rd year of his ministry. Licensed as a Minister of the Presbyterian Church in Ireland in 1956 he was ordained as Minister of Raphoe in the Presbytery of Donegal in 1961. After receiving a unanimous call from 1st Kilraughts on 14th September 1971 he was installed as minister on 16th November 1971 and remained as Minister until his retirement on 30th June 1996.

The call to a congregation who on 4th April 1971 had lost their church building as a result of fire, was a tremendous task but being a man of great discernment he saw potential and he, unlike most of us, had a vision of what the future would hold. So much so that after the first four years of his ministry, through sheer hard work, inspiration and determination, the new church and suite of buildings was dedicated to the glory of God in June 1975. Not only diligent in the oversight of the erection of the new building, Mr. Bell's preparation for the Lord's day services were conducted with dignity, clarity and brevity, with a thought provoking challenge to the member in the pew.

As a pastor he was constant in visiting – this being a feature of his ministry; many people valued his wise counsel and looked forward to his visit to their home. The congregation, although saddened at Mr. Bell's retirement in June 1996, were delighted to honour the Bell family at a Thanksgiving evening on 26th July 1996 where good wishes were conveyed for a happy retirement.

The Kirk Session was saddened to learn of the serious illness which Mrs. Bell had to contend with but we give thanks to Almighty God that health and strength had been restored in some measure to Mrs. Bell when illness struck Mr. Bell. We give thanks to God for a life of such character and usefulness, for strength, power, vision and humility. He was to us all a friend trusted, respected and loved and a true servant of our Lord Jesus Christ.

We commit to the comfort of Almighty God his wife Mrs. Roseanne Bell, daughters Patricia, Caroline and Alexandra, son-in-law Essex and grandchildren Patrick and Connor, assuring them of our prayers and knowing that they have many happy memories to cherish and treasure."[53]

Mrs. Roseanne Bell died on 9th September 2004, aged 67 years, and, after a private cremation, her ashes were also interred in First Kilraughts Churchyard.

As their headstone so eloquently records:

"In life they were loved and gracious and in death they were not parted."

After Mr. Bell's retirement, First Kilraughts congregation had to look to the future, but the people knew that, in that future, change was inevitable.

Chapter 3

Notes and References

1. Minute of Meeting of Kirk Session, 30th October 1987
2. Ibid
3. "The Chronicle", 27th Feb. 1980
4. Ibid
5. "The Chronicle", 9th March 1991
6. Ibid
7. Ibid
8. "The Chronicle", 5th March 1977
9. Ibid
10. Ibid
11. "The Chronicle", 17th October 1987
12. Ibid
13. Ibid
14. "The Chronicle", 8th January 1983
15. See details of his appointment, in Chapter 6
16. "Kilraughts: a Kirk and Its People", S.A. Blair, 1973, p.172
17. Session Minute Book (1984-2001)
18. Ibid
19. "The Chronicle," 26th February 1978
20. "Coleraine Tribune", 4th July 1984
21. Letter to present author, 19th September 1990
22. "The Radio Times", 12th January 1985
23. Finding of Presbytery of Route, Visitation of First Kilraughts, 4th and 17th April 1989
24. Ibid
25. Ibid
26. Ibid
27. Letter from Rev. W.J. Watson to Mr. S.A. Blair, 9th Jan 1996
28. Ibid
29. Ibid
30. Ibid
31. Minute of Meeting of Kirk Session, 27th May 1988
32. Minute of Meeting of Kirk Session, 13th March 1994
33. "The Chronicle," 22nd April 1978
34. Ibid
35. Ibid
36. Ibid
37. Ibid

38. Ibid
39. Ibid
40. "The Chronicle, 28th April 1979
41. Ibid
42. Ibid
43. "Northern Constitution", 16th September 1995
44. Ibid
45. Minutes of Meeting of Kirk Session, 12th February 1996
46. Ibid
47. Ibid
48. "The Chronicle," 3rd August 1996
49. Ibid
50. Ibid
51. Ibid
52. Ibid
53. Ibid
54. Minute of Meeting of Kirk Session, 1st November 200

Chapter 4

A FATHER FIGURE

During the first fourteen years of Mr. Bell's ministry in First Kilraughts, the congregation had also a Senior Minister or Minister Emeritus. The Rev. Francis Alexander Robinson, as we saw in Chapter I, retired on 31st December 1970 and he and Mrs. Robinson went to live in Postboy's Walk in Ballymoney. They were both highly esteemed in the congregation and Mr. Robinson was a father figure in Kilraughts for the rest of his life. Also, he became 'Father of the General Assembly,' the title given to the oldest minister of the Presbyterian Church in Ireland.

Although Mrs. Ruth Robinson had suffered a stroke some time before they vacated the Manse, she recovered well and was able to enjoy entertaining visitors in their new home. They liked to have members of the congregation and other friends for morning coffee or supper in the evening. It was a happy place to go with a warm and friendly atmosphere and plenty of chat and laughter. They, in turn, were often invited to members' homes and they looked forward to that, for they enjoyed keeping up their friendships and hearing all the news of what was happening in Kilraughts.

They attended worship in First Ballymoney Church and were readily welcomed into the fellowship of that congregation, many of whose members they knew well. At the same time, the happiest of relationships existed between Mr. Bell and Mr. Robinson. They enjoyed a warm and close friendship, with mutual respect for each other. Mr. Bell kept Mr. Robinson abreast of all the plans for the new church and Mr. Robinson took part in the Laying of the Foundation Stone and Opening Services. He attended all important events in the life of the congregation and often supplied the pulpit when Mr. Bell was on holiday.

GOLDEN JUBILEE

Mr. Robinson achieved an important milestone in his life in 1980. He had been ordained and installed in First Kilraughts on 28th May 1930 and on 30th May 1980 he was guest of honour at a special celebration of his Golden Jubilee as a minister of the Presbyterian Church in Ireland. His wife, family and a large number of friends joined First Kilraughts congregation to mark the event at a huge gathering in the church hall, presided over by the Rev. Robin Bell.

All were welcomed by the Clerk of Session, Mr. Andrew McR. Brown, and many tributes were paid.

The Mayor of Ballymoney, Councillor Mrs. M. J. Holmes, O.B.E. brought the congratulations of the citizens of the borough to Mr. Robinson, She paid tribute to his work in First Kilraughts and in the wider community of the borough area. The Rev. A.W.E. Forbes, senior minister of Kirkpatrick Memorial Church, Belfast, spoke on behalf of Mr. Robinson's ministerial friends. He said that his wife and he regarded Mr. and Mrs. Robinson as their closest and best friends and Mr. Forbes reminisced on humorous incidents which had taken place during the forty-six years they had known each other. The Rev. H.B. Wallace, Bushmills, Moderator of the Route Presbytery, brought the greetings and congratulations of the Presbytery. The Rev. J.G. Leitch, senior minister of Bushvale and Clerk of Presbytery, read the tribute to Mr. Robinson, which had been inserted in the Presbytery minutes, and brought the good wishes of neighbouring colleagues.

Speaking on behalf of the congregation of First Kilraughts, Mr. S. Alex. Blair, the present author, said the task which confronted Mr. Robinson when he arrived in the congregation was a very great one. 'Congregational life was very different then from now,' Mr. Blair observed, and elaborated by explaining that 50 years ago Kilraughts had 'no church hall, no organisations and no Morning Sunday school.' He continued:

'When you add to that no hymns, no paraphrases, no organ, no electricity, virtually no cars and certainly no car park, you begin to sense something of the time-span which Mr. Robinson represents in the history of this place. By the building of this Church Hall and the implementing of change after change, Mr. Robinson persevered on and successfully brought his people abreast of the times. He made First Kilraughts appreciative of the changing patterns of the church's worship and witness in the 20th century.'[1]

Mr. Blair paid tribute to Mr. Robinson's friendly nature, his tact, his sense of humour, his love of music, his ability as a pianist. As a pastor, he said, he visited the homes of the congregation with great regularity, and as a minister, he preached a gospel which was relevant and practical, and at the same time 'enabled us to touch that which is intangible, and to comprehend something of the mystery and greatness of God.'

Speaking of Mrs. Robinson, Mr. Blair said they all admired her ability as an organiser and hostess, her charm, and her hard work, which made such a contribution to the life of First Kilraughts congregation. He concluded by saying that the night was truly a 'big night' in First Kilraughts and expressed on behalf of the congregation the regard, esteem and affection in which both Mr. and Mrs. Robinson were held by all. He also expressed good wishes to them for the years to come.

PRESENTATIONS

Presentations were then made on behalf of the congregation to Mr. and Mrs. Robinson. Mr. W. Arthur Tweed presented Mr. Robinson with an inscribed gold wrist watch, and a cheque was presented by Mr. Robert Patterson. Mrs. Marion G. Sayers presented Mrs. Robinson with a pressure cooker and Mrs. Roseanne Bell presented a bouquet on behalf of the congregation.

The Rev. F.A. Robinson is presented with an inscribed gold watch by Mr. W. Arthur Tweed and a cheque by Mr. Robert Patterson to celebrate his Golden Jubilee in First Kilraughts, 30th May, 1980. Also included is the Rev. Robin Bell

Mrs. Ruth E. Robinson receives gifts from Mrs. Marion G. Sayers, the Rev. Robin Bell and Mrs. Roseanne Bell, 30th May, 1980. It was Mrs. Robinson's last time to be in First Kilraughts

Group at the Celebration of the Rev. F.A. Robinson's Golden Jubilee in First Kilraughts, 30th May, 1980 Mr. and Mrs. Robinson's family are in the back row with Mr. W.A. Tweed and Mr. Robert Patterson. Front row (left to right): The Rev. A.W.E. Forbes, Mrs. Roseanne Bell, Mr. Andrew McR. Brown, Mr. S. Alex. Blair, the Rev. Robin Bell, Mrs. Marion G. Sayers, Mrs. Ruth E. Robinson, the Rev. F.A. Robinson, Councillor Mrs. M. J. Holmes, O.B.E., the Rev. H.B. Wallace and the Rev. J.C. Leitch

Mrs. Robinson thanked the congregation for their kindness and said how much she had enjoyed living in the Manse and how greatly she valued the many friendships she made in Kilraughts.

When Mr. Robinson rose to make his reply, he received a standing ovation. He thanked the congregation for their 'lovely and useful' gifts and he went on:

> 'This is a wonderful night for me, and I have so much cause for thankfulness for being spared so long'.[2]

He said how pleased he was to have his wife and family and so many of his friends with him. He observed:

> 'Fifty years is a long time to look forward to, but, believe me, it seems a much shorter time to look back on.'[3]

He said he remembered well the Sunday morning in 1939 when, just before going out to Sunday School, he heard Mr. Chamberlain announce that 'we were at war with Germany.' He remembered, as he put it, 'the anxiety and sorrow, the prisoners-of-war and soldiers in our district, the knittings and socials, the laughter and the tears, the courtings and the weddings, and, at last, the homecomings and the rejoicing.'

Mr. Robinson recalled that visiting the congregation was always a great delight to him. He said: 'Many a time I looked forward to September when I started my regular visitation,' and added that during the years he heard some quaint sayings and had many amusing experiences. After outlining some of these, and paying a tribute to his wife, and his successor in First Kilraughts, the Rev. Robin Bell, Mr. Robinson concluded:

> 'You have a lovely church and ancillary rooms, and the spire pointing upwards can be seen for miles around. May Mr. Bell and his staff of helpers continue to lead men and women in the right direction and point them to Him who is the author and finisher of our faith.'[4]

It was fitting, because of Mr. Robinson's long connection with Ballymoney and District Male Voice Choir, that the choir should provide the main part of the entertainment. Under their conductor, Mr. T. D. McNeilly, and with Mr. Robinson accompanying them on the piano, the choir sang two groups of songs. There was also a piano duet by Mr. Robinson's two grandsons, Stephen and Shaun Gillespie, Londonderry, which was greatly appreciated by the audience.

A vote of thanks to the entertainers and to the ladies who provided supper, was proposed by the Rev. Dr. J.A. McFarland, who recalled that Mr. Robinson had preached at his ordination in Toberkeigh Church on 28th April, 1931. The evening concluded with the Benediction pronounced by Mr. Robinson.

Mr. Robinson began his fifty-first year in Kilraughts by conducting morning service in the church the following Sunday morning. He addressed a large congregation, taking as his text the words from verse 4 of the 100th Psalm: 'Enter into his gates with thanksgiving, and into his courts with praise.' The soloist was Mrs. Kathleen Barr and Mr. Howard Gillespie was guest organist. The service also commemorated the fifth anniversary of the opening and dedication of the church buildings. Rev. J. Trevor Magowan, minister of St. James's Church, Ballymoney conducted the evening service.

MODERATOR VISITED

Mr. Robinson received many messages of congratulations and, a few days after the main celebrations, the Moderator of the General Assembly, the Rt. Rev. Dr. W.M. Craig and Mrs. Craig called on Mr. and Mrs. Robinson at their home in Ballymoney.

Later in the column 'Out and About' in the 'News Letter' Mr. Robinson's notable anniversary was given mention and the columnist said it was wonderful that he was able to celebrate the beginning of his 51st year in the ministry…

'in the way he knows best – by conducting the morning service.'[5]

The writer went on:

'First Kilraughts congregation is one of the oldest in North Antrim and a look at the history books will confirm that it is a church famed for its lengthy ministries. Mr. Robinson's two predecessors were Rev. Samuel Finlay who was minister from 1850 – 1885 and Rev. John McCammon who was minister from 1887 – 1929. So for the past 130 years the First Kilraughts congregation, which dates back to the 17th century, has had only three ministers.'[6]

The article also referred to another celebration, noting:

'A gifted musician – Mr. Robinson also celebrates his 25th anniversary as accompanist to the Ballymoney and District Male Voice Choir this year, and has been given a presentation at their annual concert.'[7]

Mr. Robinson's Golden Jubilee was a memorable event in the history of First Kilraughts. It was also the last major function which Mrs. Robinson was able to attend. Her health deteriorated and she soon required full-time nursing care. She became a resident at the Model Nursing Home in Ballymoney and remained there for the rest of her life, actually outliving her husband by almost seven months.

DIAMOND JUBILEE

Few ministers have the pleasure of celebrating their Golden Jubilee in the ministry but fewer still live to celebrate their Diamond Jubilee. Mr. Robinson was spared to complete sixty years in First Kilraughts and remained erect, mobile and in good spirits, always with his famous beaming smile. He lived in Abbeyfield for a little while and then went to the Court Nursing Home where he spent his final years. He still played the piano, loved to be taken out and often entertained his friends to meals in local hotels.

When First Kilraughts congregation realised his Diamond Jubilee was approaching, the members were determined that such a unique occasion should have a special celebration. At an informal meeting of Kirk Session before the noon service on Sunday, 7th January, 1990, the present author suggested that it might be appropriate to name the church hall the Robinson Hall to mark the occasion. This was agreed unanimously by all present. The building of the hall had been Mr. Robinson's first major project soon after he arrived in Kilraughts.

The congregation had to sanction such a change and, after due announcements on two successive Sundays, a congregational meeting was held after the service on Sunday, 21st January, 1990. The Session Minute Book recorded:

> "The Rev. R. Bell presided and the Clerk (the present author) outlined the Session's proposals to name the church hall the Robinson Hall. He moved that the congregation agree to the proposal and Mr. S. Archibald seconded. It was passed unanimously, with acclamation.'[8]

Session then proceeded with further arrangements for the special celebration. These included the unveiling of a plaque by Mr. Robinson at a special service and a special lunch on the Celebration Day, Sunday 10th June, with Mr. Robinson as guest of honour. The Session Minute Book gave details of further arrangements:

> 'Session agreed that the gift of a watercolour painting (by Jack Wilkinson) of the former church building should be presented to the Rev. F.A. Robinson at the ceremonies on 10th June. On that occasion Mr. Robinson had indicated he would preach the sermon

The Rev. F.A. Robinson with, on his left, his daughter Valerie and, on his right, his two sons Frank and Richard and surrounded by their families on the 60th Anniversary of his Ordination, 10th June, 1990

The Rev. F.A. Robinson with his closest friend in the ministry, the Rev. A.W.E. Forbes, senior minister of Kirkpatrick Memorial Church, Belfast, and formerly of Roseyards, at his 60th Anniversary Celebrations

and the newly-appointed Moderator of the General Assembly, the Rt. Rev. Principal Finlay Holmes would be present and take part'.[9]

The special Diamond Jubilee Service took place, as arranged, on Sunday 10th June 1990 with great numbers attending. There was a large representation of the Robinson family, including Mr. and Mrs. Robinson's daughter Valerie and their two sons, Frank and Richard with their families, many grandchildren, and one great grand-daughter. There were also many ministerial colleagues, guests and friends, together with members of the First Kilraughts congregation.

A welcome was extended to all by the present author, Mr. S. Alex Blair, who especially welcomed the Moderator of the General Assembly, the Right Rev. Principal R.F.G. Holmes and Mrs. Josephine Holmes. He said that it was appropriate that Principal Holmes's moderatorial year should begin in Kilraughts, for his roots lay there, in places like Ganaby and Magherone. First Kilraughts was the congregation in which Principal Holmes's mother and father were brought up, and where both his grandfathers, Richard Gregg and Robert Holmes were esteemed elders. He welcomed him as 'a grandson of First Kilraughts,' and thanked him for coming, 'after an extremely busy and tiring week at the Assembly.'

The service was conducted by Rev. Robin Bell, who also gave the children's address. The lessons were read by Miss Margaret Kennedy and Mr. Frank McClure, Lisboy, and the guest soloist was Dr. Pamela Douglas, sister of the celebrated international pianist, Mr. Barry Douglas, and girl-friend of one of Mr. Robinson's grandsons. The organist was Mr. Maurice Christie and the church choir led the praise, many of the hymns sung being favourites of Mr. Robinson.

In his sermon, Mr. Robinson said he still vividly remembered the first time he preached in First Kilraughts Church and he believed that throughout his ministry he never made an enemy. He had baptised and married many of those present and he called upon all, not only to make that day one of special celebration, but also of re-dedication to God and to His church.

The Moderator of the General Assembly, Rt. Rev. Principal Finlay Holmes, thanked Mr. Robinson for such a fine and inspiring sermon and said it was really quite unique for a minister not only to be spared to celebrate the 60th anniversary of his ordination, but also to be able to preach on that day. Principal Holmes said Mr. Robinson had still the diction, dignity and clarity of exposition, which he remembered when brought as a child to First Kilraughts, when spending his holidays with his grand-parents at Ganaby. Principal Holmes then led the congregation in prayers of thanksgiving and intercession.

The Rev. F.A. Robinson unveils the commemorative plaque to record the Church Hall being named the Robinson Hall on the 60th Anniversary of his Ordination in First Kilraughts, Sunday, 10th June, 1990. With him are (left to right): The Rev. R. McC. Bell, the Rt. Rev. Professor Finlay Holmes and Mr. S. Alex. Blair

After the Benediction, pronounced by Mr. Robinson, those who had taken part in the service, accompanied by the Kirk Session and committee and sixteen people who had been present at Mr. Robinson's ordination service and followed by all present, proceeded to the vestibule. At the entrance to the church hall, Mr. Robinson was invited by Mr. Bell to name the building, 'The Robinson Hall' and to unveil a commemorative plaque. The prayer of dedication was offered by the Moderator of the General Assembly, Principal Holmes.

The plaque was inscribed:

"The Robinson Hall

This hall was named in honour of the

60th Anniversary of the Ordination of

The Reverend Francis Alexander Robinson B.A.

And in recognition of the devoted service of

Mr. Robinson and Mrs. Ruth E. Robinson

to First Kilraughts.

28th May 1990"

A congregational luncheon, prepared by the ladies of the First Kilraughts, followed in the Robinson Hall. Mr. Bell presided and welcomed all present. He spoke of all the support and encouragement he and Mrs. Bell had received from Mr. and Mrs. Robinson since coming to Kilraughts. He said this was a very special day for the congregation and he spoke of his friendship with the Moderator of the General Assembly and Mrs. Holmes. Mr. Bell then made a presentation to Principal and Mrs. Holmes and Mrs. Roseanne Bell presented Mrs. Holmes with an arrangement of flowers for the Moderator's mother, Mrs. Sophia Holmes (formerly Gregg of Magherone or Toberbilly as it is known today). Mrs. Holmes, senior, was

The Rev. F.A. Robinson with those who had been present at his Ordination and were present at the 60th Anniversary, 10th June, 1990. Front row (left to right): Miss A.M. McClure, Miss Matilda Robinson, Mrs. Mary Lyle, Miss Marion Tweed, Mrs. Sarah Brown and Mrs. Nellie Munnis. At the back (left to right): Mr. John McClure, Mrs. Eileen Losty, Miss Lily McClure, Miss Julia Tweed, Mrs. Mina Moore, Mrs. Lil McQuiston, Mr. R.J. McClure, Mrs. Hannah McIlhatton, Mr. Wm. Kirkpatrick and Miss Mary Mayberry

brought up in the congregation and was then in her ninety-eighth year. She lived to see the century and beyond.

Mrs. Josephine Holmes returned thanks for the gift which she had received but she said she was especially touched by the thoughtfulness of the congregation in sending flowers to her mother-in-law. She said Mrs. Holmes, senior, still spoke often of her love of Kilraughts and retained a strong interest in what was happening in the church and the district. Mrs. Holmes concluded by saying she and her husband were delighted that the first engagement of their moderatorial year was in Kilraughts, a place where Finlay had such strong roots and a place they both held in esteem.

136

Mr. S. Alex. Blair presents the congregation's gift to the Rev. F.A. Robinson at the 60th Anniversary Celebrations, 10th June, 1990. It was a watercolour painting by Jack Wilkinson of the Church in which Mr. Robinson preached for his entire ministry

Mrs. Roseanne Bell presents a gift of flowers to Mrs. Holmes at Mr. Robinson's 60th Anniversary Celebrations. Also included are the Rt. Rev. Professor Finlay Holmes and the Rev. Robin Bell

The Moderator then addressed the gathering and brought the greetings of the General Assembly to Mr. Robinson and to Mr. and Mrs. Bell and the congregation. He said Kilraughts was a place he had heard of from his earliest days. His parents often spoke of the Rev. John McCammon, the minister who preceded Mr. Robinson. Mr. Robinson had brought the congregation to the 20th century and now they were almost in the 21st century. Kilraughts continued to pioneer developments and to be a congregation open to change and new ideas. The Rev. Thomas Leslie went from Kilraughts as a pioneer missionary to Jamaica before the first missionaries were sent out by the first General Assembly. Kilraughts, from that early moment, remained a congregation where support for missions was strong. Throughout Mr. Robinson's ministry that enthusiasm was maintained and 'so it continues today,' said Principal Holmes. He spoke in the highest terms of Mr. and Mrs. Robinson's work in Kilraughts and commended the present minister, office bearers and people for all they were doing.

Speaking on behalf of the congregation, the present author said they felt it was appropriate that the hall should be named the Robinson Hall, for its building had been Mr. Robinson's first major project in the congregation. He had collected most of the money for it and the first social event held in it was a presentation of gifts to Mr. and Mrs. Robinson on the occasion of their marriage.

Mr. Blair said Mr. and Mrs. Robinson had served the congregation faithfully. Mrs. Robinson was a gracious hostess in the Manse, President of the W.M.A. later the P.W.A., and Leader of the Girls' Auxiliary. She was interested in every person and everything going on in the congregation. Mr. Robinson, like his wife, was greatly valued. He had given his life to the work of teacher, preacher and pastor amongst the people of Kilraughts and he had endeared himself to them in other ways – most especially for his great gift of friendship and his sense of fun.

Mr. Blair went on:

> "Here in Kilraughts he is a venerable figure, greatly beloved and greatly esteemed, but never unapproachable. His work has enriched the lives of so many and this celebration is our way of sharing in the rejoicing at such a special anniversary. I know I speak for every member of First Kilraughts and for all the guests when I say, 'thank you' to Mr. and Mrs. Robinson for their work here, and offer them congratulations on this wonderful day."[10]

Mr. Blair then presented Mr. Robinson with a gift on behalf of the congregation. It was a painting in water-colour by Mr. Jack Wilkinson of the former First Kilraughts church, in which Mr. Robinson spent his entire active ministry.

Mrs. Bell presented flowers to Mrs. Valerie Gillespie for her mother. Mrs. Gillespie returned thanks on her mother's behalf and said how much the family appreciated the many visits which members of the congregation made to her mother. Their friendship meant much to her. Her mother enjoyed being the minister's wife in First Kilraughts, took an enthusiastic and leading part in the congregational activities and was very sorry she was not able to be with them that day.

Mr. Robinson thanked the congregation for their gift and the speakers for the tributes they had paid to him. It was a memorable day for him and he was grateful to all who had been involved in making it so special. He spoke of the friendship and kindness of the Moderator's grandparents at Ganaby, and reminisced about many events and personalities of his long ministry.

Mr. Frank Robinson, Ballymena, on behalf of the Robinson family and all the guests, expressed thanks for the beautiful meal which they had enjoyed so much. He too recalled events and personalities of his days in Kilraughts. Mrs. Bell replied on behalf of the ladies.

Mr. Graham Robinson, Congregational Secretary, read a list of apologies for absence at the beginning of proceedings and the historic occasion was concluded with the Benediction, pronounced by the Moderator of the General Assembly, the Right Rev. Principal R.F.G. Holmes.

What a unique and memorable occasion it was for all who were present. As one man said:

> "It will hardly ever happen again. It is the kind of thing you tell to your grandchildren."[11]

The Rev. F.A. Robinson was to live for another four and a half years. He continued to enjoy his outings and his visitors and remained active until a short time before his death. His last time in Kilraughts was as a guest at the senior citizens' Christmas Tea in December 1994. He died at the Court Nursing Home, Ballymoney on Wednesday, 4th January 1995, in the ninety-second year of his age and the sixty-fifth of his ministry.

FUNERAL

His funeral was on Friday, 6th January 1995. After a family service in Ballymoney, conducted by the Rev. Robin Bell, the cortege made its way via Kilraughts Manse, where it made a brief stop, to First Kilraughts Church. The church was filled to capacity with a wide representation of the people of North Antrim, including many ministerial colleagues and leaders of public life.

At the church the remains were received by the officiating ministers and the Kirk Session of First Kilraughts. The coffin was carried into the church by members of the family and the Rev. Robin Bell conducted the service, all of which had been planned according to instructions left by Mr. Robinson. The two items of praise were his favourites 'The Lord's My Shepherd' and

'When I Survey The Wondrous Cross'. The church choir led the singing, as he had requested, with Mr. Maurice Christie at the organ. He had chosen as the scripture readings, passages from Psalm 90 and John's Gospel chapter 14 and these were read by the Rev. Noble McNeely, minister of First Presbyterian Church, Ballymoney. Mr. McNeely also expressed his congregation's sympathy to the Robinson family. He said how happy First Ballymoney had been to have Mr. Robinson worshipping with them for 24 years and how supportive and encouraging he had always been.

The present author was honoured to fulfill Mr. Robinson's wishes by giving a personal tribute to him. This tribute was later published, at the request of the congregation, and it is here reproduced in full:

> "In a ministry of forty and a half years and a retirement of over twenty-four years, the Rev. F.A. Robinson spent a lifetime here in North Antrim. He loved the place and its people and especially this place, First Kilraughts, and the people of this congregation. They were his people and he always brightened considerably and became especially alert when he heard the name 'Kilraughts' mentioned. He liked nothing better than to be here, to talk of this place or to talk with Kilraughts folk, many of whom kept their links with him and visited him regularly, which he and his family much appreciated.
>
> But he was in origins a city man, although both his parents were of country stock. He came from Belfast and was ordained in First Kilraughts on 28th May 1930.
>
> There is a huge vista of years between that date and today. It was a different age and a different world in 1930, and although he was of that age and that world, it did not prevent him from moving forward to accept new ways, new ideas, new initiatives. Indeed in this

141

congregation he was very much an agent for change. He pioneered the building of the church hall in 1933, now so fittingly named the Robinson Hall to honour his contribution and that of his wife to the work of this congregation. The hall enabled the congregation to develop a social dimension and new organisations and activities became possible. He introduced the organ, as was natural for a man with such a love of music and who was such a fine accompanist himself. He started the congregation singing paraphrases and then hymns and he was the first minister to wear a gown in First Kilraughts. None of these changes were effected without opposition but he had the diplomacy and the tact to handle difficulties which arose and the courage of his convictions to move forward and to bring his people with him.

Of course, first and foremost, the Rev. F.A. Robinson was a minister of the Gospel, a preacher, teacher and pastor. We can recall the clarity of his diction, the dignity with which he conducted worship, the beauty and tenderness of his prayers and his carefully prepared sermons – full of apt illustrations, garnered over the years from his well-stored mind and his wide reading. Often pointed, often challenging and always re-assuring and uplifting, he preached a message for his time based on principles which had stood the test of time and were steadfast and secure. Those of us who heard him Sunday by Sunday were taught in easily-digestible form the great truths of our faith and had revealed to us the loving kindness and tender mercy of God our Father and Jesus Christ, our Saviour and Lord.

But it was as a pastor that the Rev. F.A. Robinson did a very special work. Like his successor, the Rev. Robin Bell, he was a great visitor and, in his early days, when the countryside was full of characters, he richly enjoyed the things they said to him and the strange situations in which he sometimes found himself. Greatly gifted as a conversationalist himself and with a keen sense of humour, he could put people at their ease. He was always greeted as a friend in every home. As one lady said to me, "Ye never thought a thing about him coming in, he was no stranger, just one of ourselves".

What a lovely tribute and certainly for many his beaming smile lit up the dark moments and gave new hope. His humour diffused many a tense situation and the fact that he was there, standing with his people,

The Rev. Francis Alexander Robinson, B.A.
Ordained and Installed, 28th May, 1930
Retired, 31st December, 1970
Died, 4th January, 1995

meant so much in times of joy and celebration as well as in moments of trouble and distress. His natural love for people shone through and his encyclopaedic mind knew every family, all its ramifications, each person in that family from the oldest to the youngest – and their names would trip off his tongue without a moment of hesitation. He had a special love for the young folk and he was never happier than when they were around him in the Manse or here at church. At the Sunday School Party each year he organized the games and played the piano all night and thoroughly enjoyed himself.

In the midst of such a busy life, he also found time to teach in Dalriada School and to be the accompanist of the Ballymoney and District Male Voice Choir.

In retirement he was greatly shocked when in April 1971 the lovely old church in which he had preached for so many years was burned in an accidental fire. But he was delighted with the beauty and atmosphere of this new building which he greatly admired and in which he preached for the last time on the 60th Anniversary of his Ordination – neither a day nor a sermon which those of us who were present will ever forget. His wife's illness was also a sad disappointment to him and he bestowed much care and love on her. Their house in Postboy's Walk became, as the Manse had been, a happy place of warm hospitality and friendship for all who visited there.

In Kilraughts the Rev. F.A. Robinson had become in latter years a father or maybe even a grandfather figure. He had baptised most of the congregation including many of the elders and office holders – and it just seemed to us that he was always there – that tall erect figure, ready with the handshake, the smile and the greeting. But an era has come to an end. Today we lay him to rest in his beloved Kilraughts amongst his own Kilraughts folk.

To Mrs. Robinson, who supported him so much, we send our special thoughts today. To Frank and Doris, to Valerie and Hugh, to Richard and Pamela and their families – and how proud he was not only of his family, but of his grandchildren and especially his great grandchildren – we extend our sincere sympathy in the knowledge that they have so many happy and lovely memories to cherish and treasure.

"Grand vision of a glad new time was his;
But while he halted in the longsome years,
God called him from the life that is
And crowned him with his peers.
There on the high reaches where the view is broad,
Freed from the mists that lower landscapes mar,
He sees at last the whole intent of God
In earth and sun and star."
And to God be the glory."

The Rev. Robin Bell gave the address. He took as his text words from the 14th chapter of John's Gospel where Jesus said: "Because I love, you will love also." He said that the life which was personified in Christ and which was preached and lived by the Rev. F.A. Robinson had left a lasting mark on the people of Kilraughts. "The strength and power and vitality of his character", Mr. Bell said, "remain in each one here".

Mr. Bell described Mr. Robinson as:

"Quite simply the kindest, gentlest and most helpfully encouraging of colleagues – a senior minister who made it easy to be his successor."[12]

Mr. Bell concluded by saying that Mr. Robinson had proved himself to be:

"a staunch and true friend, the truest of the true servants of the Lord Jesus Christ."[13]

The Moderator of the General Assembly, the Rt. Rev. Dr. David J. McGaughey, offered the sympathy of the entire Presbyterian Church to Mrs. Robinson, Frank, Valerie and Richard and their families and the minister and congregation of First Kilraughts. He said it was a sad loss when 'the Father of the General Assembly' died and the whole church felt grieved by the loss. Dr. McGaughey spoke of Mr. Robinson as one who loved the Presbyterian Church, defended its principles and doctrines and taught what the church held dear. He said Mr. Robinson was a good minister of Jesus Christ, a wise counsellor and a friend, trusted, respected and loved. He then led the congregation in prayer.

The coffin was borne from the church by the family, elders of the congregation and close friends.

In the churchyard the scripture reading was by the Rev. J. Herman Brown, senior minister of Dunloy, one of Mr. Robinson's closest friends. Mr. Bell officiated at the committal and the final prayers were led by the Rev. Stephen Carson, minister of Dunluce and Moderator of the Route Presbytery.

Afterwards all present were entertained to tea in the Robinson Hall. The Moderator of the General Assembly, Dr. David McGaughey, expressed thanks to the ladies of First Kilraughts for their "kindness and hospitality."

TRIBUTE AT SUNDAY SERVICE

On the following Sunday, 8th January 1995, at the service in First Kilraughts, Mr. Bell referred to the death of the Rev. F.A. Robinson.

Preaching from the text: "Hold fast to that which is good" (Romans 12:9), Mr. Bell spoke of the Christian love, goodwill, tolerance, friendship and compassion which were evident in Mr.

Robinson's life. He went on:

> "It showed itself in any number of ways and like a lamp or a beacon of light, it shone through every period of his life. His interest in and love for this congregation, so well-known while he laboured here, remained undiminished and undimmed during all the twenty-four years of retirement. He was a master of the art of Christian living, an art which he demonstrated in a life of self-effacing humility, devotion to duty and love towards God and the people of God in this place. What a splendid example for each of us to follow."[14]

Mr. Bell offered prayers of thanksgiving for Mr. Robinson's life and work and prayers of comfort for his wife and family.

It may be a cliché, but it was truly the end of an era in First Kilraughts. Mr. Robinson had been a corner-stone of the place for sixty-four and a half years. Everyone felt diminished by his passing, for he had touched the lives of everyone in so many ways over such a long expanse of time.

DEATH OF MRS RUTH E. ROBINSON

Mrs. Ruth Emily Robinson died at the Model Nursing Home in Ballymoney on 9th August 1995. Her funeral, which was to First Kilraughts Churchyard, was "strictly private"[15] but later an appreciation of her life was published in the local paper. It is reproduced here in full:

> "Mrs. Ruth Robinson, widow of the late Rev. F.A. Robinson, died peacefully after a long illness which she bore courageously and without complaint.
>
> She was born in 1910, the youngest daughter of Mr. John Moffett of Buxton House, Cork City and, after sacrificing an academic career in order to look after her widowed father, she came the length of Ireland in 1933 to marry Alex Robinson, minister of First Kilraughts

Presbyterian Church. So began a 60 year partnership, in the course of which she raised a family and acted as a perfect companion and complement to her husband in the work of the church and in the life of the community.

Having been actively involved in working with youth as a Girl Guide captain in Cork, she turned her energies to the formation in the church of a branch of the Girls' Auxiliary. She revitalised the Women's Missionary Association, of which she was congregational president from 1934 until 1970. She taught in the Sunday School and she was a member of the church choir, where she gave a lead with her strong contralto voice. In this, as in all that she did, she led by quiet example. She never lost her soft southern accent and, although she preferred to work in the background, in an unostentatious way, her energetic ever-active involvement and enthusiasm infected those around her.

She was a devoted mother and later took great pleasure in her eight grand-children, whom she, in turn, introduced to her pleasure in bathing, picnicing, nature and outdoor things in general.

Sadly, and particularly so for an energetic woman who filled all her waking hours in an active way, she suffered a disabling stroke at the age of 59 but battled against adversity, persisted daily with physiotherapy exercises, recovered her speech and learned to do much, including writing with her left hand. Such was her recovery that, with her husband's help, she managed to run her new home in Ballymoney for almost 20 years and maintained contact with a wide circle of friends. Even in her final pain-filled years, she endeared herself to those who cared so well for her and who, with family and surviving friends, will sadly miss her."[16]

PIANO – A MEMORIAL GIFT

On Sunday, 17th September 1995 at a special Service of Remembrance of the Rev. F.A. and Mrs. R.E. Robinson, held in First Kilraughts, the Robinson family presented to the congregation the very appropriate gift of a piano for use in the church as a memorial to their parents. Present were Mr.

The Robinson Family photographed at the piano which they presented in memory of their parents, the Rev. F.A. Robinson and Mrs. R.E. Robinson, Sunday, 17th September, 1995. Seated are Mrs. Doris Robinson and Mrs. Valerie Gillespie. Standing are Mr. Richard Robinson, Mr. Frank Robinson, Mrs. Pamela Robinson and Mr. Hugh Gillespie

The Robinson Family and those who took part in the Dedication of the piano in memory of the Rev. F.A. and Mrs. R.E. Robinson, 17th September, 1995. The Dedication was performed by the Very Rev. Dr. A.W. Godfrey Brown, Ballycastle

and Mrs. Robinson's daughter, Mrs. Valerie Gillespie, and her husband, Mr. Hugh Gillespie, Londonderry, together with Mr. and Mrs. Robinson's two sons, Mr. Frank Robinson, Ballymena and his wife Doris and Mr. Richard Robinson, Carrickfergus, and his wife Pamela. Also present were twelve grandchildren and great-grandchildren of Mr. and Mrs. Robinson.

The lessons were read by Mr. Frank Robinson and Mr. Alex Blair and the memorial gift was received on behalf of the congregation by the minister of First Kilraughts, the Rev. Robin Bell, who conducted the service. It was dedicated by the Very Rev. Dr. A.W. Godfrey Brown, minister of Ballycastle Presbyterian Church and a former Moderator of the General Assembly.

Dr. Brown was the guest preacher and paid a warm tribute to the work of Mr. and Mrs. Robinson.

Dr. Pamela Gillespie, sister of the world-acclaimed pianist, Mr. Barry Douglas, was the soloist. She was accompanied on the new piano by her husband, Mr. Shaun Gillespie, grandson of Mr. and Mrs. Robinson.

During the service, two of the Rev. F. A. Robinson's favourite hymns "When I survey the Wondrous Cross" and "How Sweet the Name of Jesus Sounds" were sung. The church choir sang the anthem "Through all the changing scenes of life" and Mr. Maurice Christie was at the organ.

Before the service, coffee was served in the Robinson Hall and members and visitors had the opportunity to meet the Robinson family and renew old friendships, as well as reminisce about the days of the ministry of the Rev. F.A. Robinson in First Kilraughts.

Chapter 4

Notes and References

1. "The Chronicle", 7th June 1980
2. Ibid
3. Ibid
4. Ibid
5. "The News Letter", 22nd August 1980
6. Ibid
7. Ibid
8. Record in Session Minute Book, 21st January 1990
9. Minute of Kirk Session, 1st April 1990
10. "The Ballymoney Times", 13th June 1990
11. Ibid
12. "The Ballymoney Times", 11th January 1995
13. Ibid
14. Ibid
15. Notice in "The News Letter", 10th August 1995
16. "The Chronicle", 19th August 1995

Chapter 5

ONWARD TO 350

This chapter brings the history of the congregation up to the present day. In so doing it is dealing with events which are fresh in the memory of many readers and involves people who are still alive. Therefore it cannot offer any historical analysis but can merely record what happened, with as much accuracy as possible. We begin in 1996 with the Rev. J.T. Magowan as convener of the vacancy.

THE VACANCY

Although minister of the largest congregation in the Route Presbytery, Mr. Magowan gave First Kilraughts a high priority in his schedule. He visited with much acceptance, ensured the pulpit was filled each Sunday by experienced and erudite preachers and was in Kilraughts as often as he could. He was diplomatic in his dealings with applicants for the vacancy and led the delegation from the congregation to the meeting of the Union Commission in Belfast. There, permission was given to call a new minister, the call figure agreed being £15,750 with £5,000 expenses.

One of the events which took place during the vacancy was a visit by the Mid-Antrim Historical Group for the launch of the second volume of the present author's series "County Antrim Characters". It took place in the Robinson Hall on Thursday 7th November 1996 and on that evening Kilraughts welcomed a large number of distinguished visitors who all made speeches, referring in the highest terms to the new publication and its author. Speakers included Dr Eull Dunlop, secretary of the Mid Antrim Historical Group, compiler and editor of the book; Mr. Maurice O'Neill, editor of the "Ballymena Guardian", in which newspaper the pen portraits had originally appeared and who had written a preface to the book; Dr. John Robb, the distinguished surgeon and Senator in the Parliament of the Irish Republic; Alderman Joseph A Gaston, M.B.E., Mayor of Ballymoney; Mrs. Mollie Holmes, O.B.E., former Mayor of Ballymoney; the Rev. Dr. Adam Loughridge, Professor of Church History and Principal of the Reformed Presbyterian Theological Hall; the Rev. Robert Hanna, minister of Kellswater R.P. Church and author of "The Armoy Athletes" and "McIlmoyle of Dervock" and Alderman Sandy Spence, M.B.E., former Mayor of Ballymena. Alderman Spence said that, in coming to Kilraughts that evening he was coming back to his roots, for his mother was "a McWilliams of Kilmoyangie" and he recalled childhood holidays at his mother's old home. Mr. James G. Kenny, the famous "Bard of Ballygarvey," was unable to be present but sent his greetings in verse as follows:

> Kilraughts it is a famous place –
> Its folk staunch rural kind.
> Attend Kirk on the Sabbath Day,
> To worship and unwind.

> They hear the sermon and the prayers,
> With gladness sing God's praise,
> For no odds what else fluctuates
> They know He always stays.

> Its history is a lengthy one,
> Compiled into a book
> By Alex Blair some years ago –
> No doubt much time it took.

> School teacher, Alex, is of course,
> So versatile indeed.
> "Thought for the Day" on radio
> His logic wise folk heed.

> People and Places he detailed,
> Were in the local press.
> Volume I has appeared in print,
> Being a great success.

Eull Dunlop a large hand played
In Volume I's debut.
Now, with his hand still on the plough,
Emerged has Volume 2.

I could rhyme on, though that's enough,
'Tis best I say no more.
Hear of Megraw's "twelve titted soo"
Then laugh till yer sides are sore!

The Rev. J. Trevor Magowan, convener of the vacancy, presided. Entertainment was provided by Television's "Singing Farmer", Mr. John Watt, and there were also songs from Mr. David Loughridge and the Kilraughts trio of Mrs. Lottie McIlhatton, Mrs. Janette Reid and Mrs. Grace Lamont. The large audience enjoyed Mrs. Heather Montgomery's violin solos and were entertained to supper by the ladies of First Kilraughts. Mr. Maurice Christie was accompanist and entertained on the piano as the audience assembled. The memorable evening was brought to a close with a vote of thanks proposed by the Rev. Ian McClean, minister of Toberkeigh Presbyterian Church, and seconded by the Rev. J. Herman Brown, senior minister of Dunloy Presbyterian Church.

The vacancy gave the opportunity to complete the work at the Manse which had been started during Mr. Bell's ministry. The committee members were glad to continue the conservation of the rest of the house and protect it from the ravages of woodworm. The firm of J.S. Dunlop re-started work in October 1996 and this included some re-roofing, picking and plastering of a number of external and internal walls, the provision of new window frames, the installation of a damp course throughout and the replacing of some of the ground floors of the house. The grounds were also tidied and re-modelled, so that the Manse would be in pristine condition for its next occupant.

It was the selection of that occupant which was uppermost in the minds of the members. The Kirk Session gave much thought, time and prayer to this process and altogether interviewed some fourteen candidates. Three were chosen to preach and this took place in February 1997. At a congregational meeting on Tuesday, 25th February 1997 the Rev. David Huey Thompson, assistant minister of Bloomfield Church, Belfast, was chosen to be the next minister of First Kilraughts.

As Mr. Thompson had obtained more than two thirds of the votes, it was agreed that the call should be made unanimous. A delegation from First Kilraughts tabled the call to Mr. Thompson at a meeting of East Belfast Presbytery in Knock Church on the evening of Tuesday, 4th March 1997. He accepted and he and his wife, Angela, took up residence in the Bregagh Manse a few days before his installation.

INSTALLATION OF THE REV. D.H. THOMPSON

David Huey Thompson is a native of Belfast, the son of Mrs. Dorothy and the late Mr. A.J. Thompson. He was brought up in Ravenhill congregation and educated at Annadale Grammar School, Grosvenor High School and the Queen's University of Belfast, from which he graduated with an honours B.A. degree. He continued his studies at Union Theological College, obtained a B.D. degree and was licensed by the Presbytery of East Belfast, becoming ordained assistant in Bloomfield Church. He was installed in First Kilraughts on Friday, 18th April 1997.

There was a packed congregation of about five hundred present for the installation service conducted by the Presbytery of Route. The Moderator of Presbytery, The Rev John T McCullough, minister of Toberdoney and Croaghmore, conducted worship and the sermon was preached by the Rev. George Cunninghan, minister of Armoy and Ramoan. The acting clerk, the Rev. Dr. R.F.S. Poots, read the Rule of Faith and Mr. Thompson, having answered the prescribed questions,

Group at the Installation of the Rev. David H. Thompson as minister of First Kilraughts, Friday, 18th April, 1997. Front row (left to right): The Rev. J.T. McCullough, Moderator of Presbytery, the Rev. David Thompson and Mr. S. Alex. Blair. Back row: The Rev. J.T. Magowan, the Rev. Dr. Derek Poots, and the Rev. Robin Bell

The Rev. Robin Bell welcomes his successor, the Rev. David Thompson, 18th April, 1997

signed the Formula of Subscription and was duly installed as minister of First Kilraughts by the Moderator, who offered the new minister the right hand of fellowship. The charge to minister and people was given by the Rev. J. Trevor Magowan and an augmented choir, with Mr. Maurice Christie at the organ, sang "O God, You search me," based on Psalm 139.

Following the service, supper was served and a reception was held in the church, presided over by the Moderator, Mr. McCullough. He welcomed Mr. and Mrs. Thompson on behalf of the Presbytery and Mr. S.A. Blair, Clerk of Session, offered a warm welcome on behalf of the congregation of First Kilraughts. Addressing Mr. Thompson, Mr. Blair said:

> "Your settlement has been a most happy one and we hope that spirit of happiness, co-operation, mutual esteem and encouragement of each other will be the hallmark of this new era in our congregation's history"[1]

Mr. Blair thanked the Rev. J.T. Magowan for all his work as convener and presented him with a painting as a token of the congregation's gratitude. Mrs. Maeve Magowan was also thanked and presented with flowers by Mrs. Annie Patterson, wife of the congregational treasurer. Mrs. Betty Robinson, wife of the congregational secretary, presented flowers to Mrs. Angela Thompson.

Speeches then followed from a number of visiting ministers. The Rev. Graham Connor, Bloomfield, Belfast, spoke highly of Mr. Thompson's time as assistant in Bloomfield. Further evidence of the esteem in which Mr. and Mrs. Thompson were held was shown by the presence of about eighty members of Bloomfield congregation, who made the journey from Belfast in a specially-chartered double decker bus. The Rev. William McKeown, Ravenhill, Belfast, brought greetings and good wishes from Mr. Thompson's home congregation, which was also well represented at the service. Also present were Mr. Thompson's mother, two sisters and relatives from County Tyrone.

A college friend, the Rev. William Henry, Maze, spoke on behalf of Mr. Thompson's fellow students. The Rev. Harry Coulter, minister of Kilraughts Reformed Presbyterian Church, proposed a vote of thanks and welcomed Mr. Thompson on behalf of neighbouring churches. Among other church representatives attending were the Very Rev. Canon Kevin Donnelly, Parish Priest, Loughgiel, and the Rev. Canon E.R. Lavery, rector of Ballymoney. Mr. Coulter's vote of thanks was seconded by Mr. Max Kernoghan, Clerk of Session, Bloomfield.

During the evening songs were enjoyed from the Kilraughts trio of Mrs. Lottie McIlhatton, Mrs. Grace Lamont and Mrs. Janette Reid. The Young People's Musical Group also played and proceedings closed with Mr. the Mrs. Thompson greeting visitors and their new congregation at the door.

THE REV. DAVID H. THOMPSON IN KILRAUGHTS

Mr. Thompson later wrote that.....

> "going to be minister of First Kilraughts exposed me to a whole new setting of rural community and church life from I had been used to as someone who grew up in Belfast."[2]

The manse was in the heart of the countryside surrounded by farms and, as he visited, he negotiated country roads and laneways, all of which was a new experience for the young minister. He sometimes found the speech of the people a little confusing but the welcome he was given was always warm and supportive. His greeting of "Hi, guys" was rather different from that with which many of his members were familiar, but he brought with him a disarming charm which soon won them over. Described as "a sensitive and delightful young man with much evangelical zeal and a powerful desire to serve his people", Mr. Thompson's youthful enthusiasm was appreciated by the congregation.

Although this was his first charge, he showed much perception and maturity in the steady and balanced way he approached his work. He knew change would come slowly and, while encouraging it, he never pushed it too far but was always aware of the need to bring his people with him.

Mr. Thompson was a gifted academic and this showed itself in the quality of his pulpit ministry. His depth of study and wide knowledge of the scriptures were evident in his sermons, which he prepared conscientiously. They were delivered with persuasive modesty and evangelical concern. During his time in First Kilraughts, Mr. Thompson gained a Master of Philosophy degree from the Queen's University of Belfast to add to the degrees he already held in Arts and Divinity. A committed student, he gave a high priority to study and research.

On the lighter side, the Rev. David Thompson was a keen football fan – a lifelong supporter of Linfield Football Club in Belfast. Most Saturdays he attended their matches and this gave him a ready point of contact with the young people – and some not-so-young – in the congregation who shared his absorbing interest. All did not support Linfield but they were able to debate with him the merits or otherwise of their respective teams and much light-hearted banter resulted.

A profile of the numbers and ages of the members to whom Mr. Thompson preached each Sunday emerged from a census of the congregation taken just a few months before he arrived. This census, on Sunday 19th January 1997, taken in churches across the country, revealed that on that Sunday, at the 12 noon service in First Kilraughts, there was an attendance of 67 males and 78 females, a total congregation of 145 people. They divided into age groups as follows.

Under 25 years:	24 males	23 females
26-55 years:	24 males	27 females
56 years and over	14 males	26 females.

Of the latter group 8 males and 22 females were over 65 years of age. 5 males and 2 females did not reveal to which age group they should be allocated. The large number of young people in the congregation augured well for the future, especially now with a new young minister.

At a meeting of Kirk Session on 16th September 1997 the Rev. David Thompson tabled a document which he entitled "Towards Maturity in Unity" outlining matters which he felt should be discussed. There were four main headings – Worship, General Church Life, Missionary Links and Interests and the need for a photocopier.

The last matter was agreed immediately, but the rest demanded more discussion and thought. However, as time went on, most of the suggestions which he put forward, came to fruition. A congregational supplement of hymns not in the hymn book came about when the booklet called "Words of Worship" appeared in June 1999. The Bible Study Group was re-launched as the Sunday Evening Fellowship, a tape ministry of the Sunday service for those who were ill or elderly and could not attend, came into being and social events were organised to bring the people together. Links with missionary organisations were fostered and worship and church life were strengthened

Guidelines for parental requirements for the baptism of children were discussed at a meeting of Kirk Session on 19th January 1998. It was agreed that at least one of the parents should be a communicant member and in regular attendance at public worship. If any problems arose these should be referred to the Session and the Session...

> "commended Mr. Thompson for his encouraging and sensitive attitude with regard to this sacrament."[3]

1998 was designated "Year of Evangelism" and First Kilraughts marked it with a number of events. Organisations which participated included the PWA and the youth groups. The men were also included, a special Men's Dinner being held in the Robinson Hall on the evening of Saturday 10th October.

Mr. and Mrs. Thompson were guests of honour at the annual Parents' Night of Kilraughts Young Farmers' Club held in the Robinson Hall in March 1999. Mr. Thompson told Session that the one-act play performed that night....

"had caused him great distress because of its content."[4]

This drew an apology from the producers and the following year the Y.F.C. sent a copy of the script of that year's play for the consideration of Mr. Thompson and the Session. On that occasion no objection was found and plays continued to be staged by the Y.F.C. in the hall with no further problems.

One of the first special events in the congregation at the beginning of Mr. Thompson's ministry was a visit to First Kilraughts by the Presbyterian Historical Society of Ireland. They were on a Field Trip to the Route, led by the present author, on Saturday 24th June 1997 and they were much impressed with the long history of the congregation and the beautiful church building.

A "big" weekend took place in the congregation at the beginning of February 2000. There was a Friday night event for the young people, an afternoon of activity for children on the Saturday and, on Saturday night, an entertainment in the Robinson Hall. The idea was to involve the entire community and encourage people to come to church. The Saturday night concert featured the distinguished Londonderry bass soloist, Mr. William Loughlin, accompanied by Mr. Adrian Anderson, and Miss Liz Weir, the well-known storyteller. The weekend concluded with two services on Sunday, 6th February, the evening service being the annual Praise Service given on that year by the Route Singers.

To celebrate the Millennium a service was held at 11.30pm on 31st December 1999 for the five local churches of Roseyards, Dervock, Bushvale, Ballyweaney and First Kilraughts. A new hymn book, "Praise" was chosen by Mr. Thompson to further augment the variety of praise selections used in the services. Copies of this book were provided for all in July 2000 due to the generosity of the Tweed family, Glennylough, and in memory of Mr. & Mrs. W. Arthur Tweed. The Kirk Session also decided on Mr. Thompson's recommendation, that the New International Version of the Bible should be used in church, but Mr. Thompson agreed also to use the Authorised Version from time to time, as appropriate.[5]

At the beginning of 1998 Mr. Tom Richmond presented a radio microphone to the congregation and this proved an asset to preachers and speakers.

PRIMARY SCHOOLS

Like his predecessors, the Rev. David Thompson was elected chairman of the Board of Governors of the two primary schools in the Kilraughts area – Knockahollet and Killyrammer. Like his predecessors he visited the schools and took assembly regularly.

Knockahollet was the larger and older of the two schools and had close links with the congregation down the generations. In the period covered by this book a number of First Kilraughts members were teachers there, most notably Miss Margaret Kennedy and also Mrs. T. L. Boyd, Mrs. Lorna McClure and Mrs. Mary Murray. The caretaker for many years was Mrs. Isobel Aiken, another member of the congregation, who was awarded the M.B.E. for her services to the school. Large numbers of children of the congregation received their early education there, and proceeded on to secondary education usually at Ballymoney High or Dalriada School.

A similar pattern prevailed at Killyrammer School but in 1997 alarm was expressed at the diminishing number of pupils on rolls there. In December 1997 the North Eastern Education and Library Board predicted it was unlikely there would be more than ten pupils attending the school in September 1998. They therefore moved to close it and this took effect from 31st August 1998. Before that, an evening was held at the school for "old" boys and girls, presided over by Mr. Thompson. Amongst the many who attended was Miss Violet E. Gilmour, who had been a teacher when the school opened on 1st April 1931. She was in the unique position of having seen both the school's opening and closing. She had taught in it for thirty-four years and her successor in charge of the infant and junior classes was Mrs. Charlotte McIlhatton, a member of First Kilraughts congregation.

AFTERNOON SUNDAY SCHOOL

Another victim of diminishing numbers was Craigatempin Sunday School, the only afternoon Sunday School remaining within the bounds of the congregation. Although independent from the control of First Kilraughts Church, many children of the congregation attended it over the years and most of the teachers were Presbyterians from First Kilraughts. Mr. Thompson, like his predecessors, was chairman of the Trustees of Craigatempin Hall, where the school was held, and in 1998 they took the decision to close the Sunday School. (For more details see Chapter 6).

VISITATION OF PRESBYTERY, SEPTEMBER 1999

A visitation of Presbytery took place in September 1999 and the statistics collected showed the number of families as 183. That amounted to a membership of about 500 persons and there were 34 children in the Sunday School with a Bible Class of 6 young people.

The organisations in the congregation were listed, with membership, as follows:

Craigatempin Hall, which was closed in 1998

Killyrammer Primary School which was also closed in 1998

Organisation	Membership
Youth Fellowship	23
Brownies	26
Boys' Brigade	37
Youth Club	30
Girls' Fellowship	36
Bowling Club	30
Badminton Club	17
Saturday Spot (Young adults)	26

The Finding paid tribute to the work of the Rev. R. McC Bell and Mrs. Bell and spoke of Mr. Thompson in the highest terms, saying...

> "he has entered his ministry with vision and enthusiasm. Gracious, capable and diligent, he enjoys the affection and esteem of his people. The standard of his life and work indicates a very successful ministry."[6]

The Commission of Presbytery saw....

> "...raising the vision and deepening the commitment of some members"[7]

... as the greatest challenge to minister and people and commended the congregation for "the loyal personal and financial support of so many members".[8] The Rev. E.J. Hyndman, Roseyards, read the Finding to the congregation.

RESIGNATION OF REV. DAVID H. THOMPSON

On 4th June 2000 Mr. Thompson informed Kirk Session that he was the sole nominee for the vacancy at Strand Church in Belfast. He preached there on Sunday 25th June and a unanimous call was issued to him. He wrote:

"Believing this to be God's will, I will be accepting the invitation, so requiring me to vacate the office of minister in First Kilraughts probably towards the end of the summer period.

Angela and I would like to thank you for your prayerful concern and support for us, especially over the past uncertain weeks and to assure you of our prayers for the congregation in these days and the days that lie ahead."[9]

Mr. Thompson preached his farewell sermon in First Kilraughts on Sunday, 13thAugust 2000. At the close of the service the present author paid tribute to Mr. Thompson's work in the congregation. He remarked:

"We have all benefitted from his explanations of the Word, especially his knack of bringing it down to simple understandable concepts and applying it to practical situations."[10]

Mr. Blair spoke of Mr. Thompson's work among the young and his regular visitation of the sick and the elderly. Referring to Mrs. Angela Thompson, he said:

"Mrs. Thompson has always been ready to play her part in the life and work of the congregation and to support her husband, as well as pursuing a busy teaching career."[11]

He concluded:

"David and Angela are both very popular and highly regarded here in First Kilraughts. We wish them well in Strand, where we hope they will be happy and fulfilled in their work. We know the blessing of God goes with them whatever the future may hold."[12]

Presentations were then made to Mr. and Mrs. Thompson. Mrs. Betty Robinson, a member of the committee, presented Mrs. Thompson with a basket of flowers and Mr. Blair presented Mr. Thompson with two water colour paintings by Ballymoney artist, Jack Wilkinson. One depicted First Kilraughts Church and the other was of a North Antrim coastal scene near Fair Head.

In his reply Mr. Thompson spoke of the kindness which he and his wife had enjoyed in First Kilraughts and said they would both have the fondest memories of the church and the people. Later Mr. Thompson wrote:

> "Please be assured of our thoughts and prayers for the congregation now and in the future. The warmth of welcome and fellowship we have enjoyed in First Kilraughts is something we will carry with us for the rest of our lives. The congregation and its people will always have a special place in our hearts."[13]

The Rev. David Thompson was installed as minister of Strand Church on 31st August 2000 and a large delegation from First Kilraughts attended the ceremony. He remained at Strand until 31st March 2008 when he resigned to become the Development Officer of the Board of Mission of the Irish Presbyterian Church, his present post.

VACANCY AGAIN

After the shortest ministry in the history of the congregation, First Kilraughts was again vacant. The Presbytery appointed the Rev. Edward J. Hyndman, minister of Roseyards, as convener and the search began for another minister. Four candidates applied and were interviewed by the Kirk Session. Two of these were invited to preach and at a congregational meeting on Monday, 21st May 2001, the Rev. Noel McClean, minister of Old Congregation Church, Randalstown, received well in excess of the two thirds majority required to become the next minister. It was agreed by all present to make the call unanimous and a delegation tabled the call to Mr. McClean at a meeting of Templepatrick Presbytery in Kilbride Church on 7th August 2001.

During the vacancy improvements were made both to the land and house at Breckagh – some fields were drained and re-seeded and an ensuite bathroom and an oil cooker were installed in the house. The place was in good order and looking well for the new Manse family.

THE REV. NOEL McCLEAN, B.Sc., Dip.Th.

The Rev. Noel McClean is a Tyrone man, born on Christmas Day 1955, and brought up on a farm near Aughnacloy. He attended Aughnacloy Primary and Secondary Schools and then went on to the Royal School, Dungannon. His education continued at what was then the Northern Ireland Polytech at Jordanstown (now part of the University of Ulster) and he graduated Bachelor of Science with Honours. As a child he went to Aughnacloy Presbyterian Church and later became a member of Dungannon church, where the minister, the Very Rev. Dr. Andrew R. Rodgers, played a large part in encouraging him to become a minister. Mr. McClean attended Union Theological College and obtained a Diploma in Theology. He was licensed by Tyrone Presbytery in Dungannon church in 1981 and on 15th January 1982 he was ordained as a Presbyterian minister and inducted as assistant to the Rev. J.A. Fullerton in Carnmoney Presbyterian church.

1983 was an important year for Mr. McClean for it was the year in which he married and was called to his first charge. On 12th February he married Miss Michele Redmond from Belfast and on 23rd February he was installed as minister of Clontibret with Middletown.

Each Sunday he had to cross the border to get to Middletown, where he was stated supply, and this was often fraught with difficulties but he enjoyed his time there. At Clontribret, amongst many improvements to all the church property, the erection of a new Church Hall in1985 gave a whole new impetus to congregational work, especially among the large numbers of youth there. In 1987 it was decided to change the arrangement between the two congregations and instead of Middletown, Mr. McClean became stated supply to Smithborough. In 1989 he was Moderator of the Synod of Dublin. On 17th October 1991 he was installed as minister of the Old Congregation, Randalstown, and remained there until his call to First Kilraughts. He came to First Kilraughts as an experienced minister and with a wife and family of four – Kathryn Elizabeth, Gemma Michele, Charis Noelle and Marcus Andrew.

INSTALLATION

A congregation of about four hundred and fifty people filled First Kilraughts Church for the installation service on Friday, 17th August 2001, conducted by the Route Presbytery.

The Moderator, the Rev. D. Ian J. McNie, Trinity, Ballymoney, led the service and the sermon was preached by the Rev. Ronald D. McDowell, Bushmills. The clerk, the Rev. H. Barclay Wallace, read the Rule of Faith and Mr. McClean, having answered the prescribed questions and signed the Formula of Subscription, was duly installed as minister of First Kilraughts by the Moderator, Mr. McNie. The charge to minister and people was given by the Rev. Edward J. Hyndman, Roseyards. The church choir, with Mr. Maurice Christie at the organ, sang the anthem "Safe in the shadow of the Lord", based on Psalm 91.

The Moderator presided at the Reception which followed. He brought the greetings and good wishes of the Presbytery of Route and of the General Assembly to the new minister and

The McClean Family. Back row: The Rev. Noel McClean, Mrs. Michele McClean, Charis McClean. Front row: Kathryn McClean, Marcus McClean and Gemma McClean.

the congregation of First Kilraughts. Mr. Arnold McClure, Clerk of Session, welcomed Mr. McClean, his wife and family, to the congregation and hoped they would feel happy in First Kilraughts. Mr. Robert Patterson, the church treasurer, made a presentation to the Rev. E.J. Hyndman, who had been convener of the vacancy. He thanked him for all his work and also thanked his wife, Mrs. Lynne Hyndman, who was presented with flowers by Mrs. Lorna McClure. Mrs. Michele McClean was also presented with flowers.

Mr. Tommy Nicholl, Clerk of Session of O.C. Randalstown, brought greetings on behalf of his congregation and spoke of the esteem in which Mr. McClean was held. This was evident by the presence of about ninety members of O.C., who had travelled from Randalstown for the service. The Very Rev. Dr. Andrew R. Rodgers, minister emeritus of Dungannon, said he had known Mr. McClean from his youth and spoke glowingly of him under the headings – person, pastor and preacher. He wished him well in his new charge. The Rev. James A. Fullerton, minister emeritus of Carnmoney relayed greetings from Carnmoney and spoke warmly of Mr. McClean's time as his assistant. The Rev. Harry Coulter, minister of Kilraughts R.P. Church, proposed a vote of thanks for the supper and brought the greetings and good wishes of the Covenanters of Kilraughts. The evening ended with Mr. and Mrs. McClean speaking to members and visitors at the door as they left at the conclusion of another memorable night in the history of First Kilraughts congregation.

The McClean family easily "settled in" and the people soon realised they had an energetic new minister with a supportive wife and children who were ready to become involved in church life. When Mr. McClean preached "on trial" many were impressed by his ability in the pulpit and this was re-enforced as time went on. It became very obvious that, with his strong clear voice, considerable rhetorical powers, and facility for apt and meaningful illustration, often drawn from his own experiences, they had acquired a minister of exceptional pulpit skills. Mr. McClean's preaching has been a characteristic of his ministry in First Kilraughts – it has been relevant, uplifting and focused. He has also the ability to make his point and not to labour it and he knows when and how to conclude.

In the general work of the congregation and its organisations he shows much expertise as an organiser and administrator. He can speedily get to the core of an issue and is decisive, balanced and confident in his leadership. This was recognised beyond the limits of the congregation when he was appointed Clerk of the Route Presbytery in 2008.

Mr. McClean enjoys life at the Manse, set amongst a farming community, with which he feels much affinity. He understands the ways of country folk but is equally at home with those whose background is in business and the professions. He has the ability to minister to all in a suitable and effective manner. He visits assiduously and, in this he has strong support from his wife, Michele, who nearly always accompanies him. The Rev. Noel McClean's ministry in First Kilraughts has shown a dynamic mixture of determination and enthusiasm with understanding, skill and diplomacy and the members are appreciative of his work amongst them.

INNOVATIONS

A number of innovations have been introduced into congregational life. These have included publication of an annual magazine called "First K. Kirk News" outlining what has happened in First Kilraughts each year. The first of these appeared in December 2001 and they have appeared each year since. Printed announcements were introduced soon after Mr. McClean's arrival and the congregation is indebted to Mrs. Michele McClean, who undertakes the printing of these each week. A week-long Holiday Bible Club was begun in August 2003 and this has been an enjoyable and happy Summer experience for young people each year ever since. The week reaches its climax with a Family Service on the concluding Sunday. Another innovation has been a Congregational Outing, the first of these taking place on the last Saturday of June 2003 with a visit to Mr. McClean's native Tyrone. These have been held in alternate years and other places visited have included Donegal and Londonderry. It was also realised that the congregation must embrace the technological age and a church website was set up by Dr. Samuel Brown. It was in place by September 2002 and has been kept updated by Mrs. Anne Richmond. A fortnightly Prayer Meeting before the service was

Holiday Bible Club, August 2005

Congregational Outing, June 2003

174

introduced in 2007 and in 2008 prayer meetings for missionary work were started in the homes of members.

In 2010 a Mission Plan was put in place. It gave the aim of the congregation as "to know Jesus and make Him known" and the Plan stated:

> "We hold firmly to the fundamental doctrines of the Christian faith, seeking to present the evangelical gospel in a winsome way, wanting to introduce people to Jesus, to find a personal faith in Him and serve Him in the community. We worship in the "simple Presbyterian style" using a variety of old and new praise items and increasingly a number of people take part in the services.
>
> We feel that we are a friendly and welcoming fellowship always looking out for new members and seeking to care spiritually for them. Some of our strengths are that we have very suitable accommodation and a large welcoming area, good music and reasonably well supported youth organisations."

The Plan concludes by saying that while the ethos of congregational life is changing, it is changing "for the better".

IMPROVEMENTS TO PROPERTY

Major improvement schemes have taken place both at the church and the manse. In 2004 a two-story extension was added to the Robinson Hall and this provided a much-needed chair store downstairs with a meeting and games room upstairs. Wheelchair access to the hall was created during Mr. Bell's ministry and now a disabled toilet was added to these facilities. In the interests of safety, iron railings were installed around the church and along all exterior flights of steps. A major and expensive project was the provision of new kitchens at the church and manse in 2006 and an open day was held at the manse on Saturday 24th June, when members were invited to inspect the new kitchen there. Many favourable comments were forthcoming. It was reported at a meeting of committee on 22nd January 2002 that 20,000 trees had been planted in five days on the manse farm in a great environmental improvement effort. In the 350th year new PowerPoint multi-media facilities have been installed in the church as an additional aid to worship.

GIFTS

A number of gifts have been presented. The present author presented a water-colour painting of the old Kilraughts Church (1820-1892) in 2002 in memory of his mother, Mrs. Mary (Mamie) Blair. Also associated with the gift were her cousins in U.S.A. A New International Version Pulpit Bible was presented on 2nd December 2001 in memory of Mr. & Mrs. James Richmond, Toberbilly. It was the gift of their sons Bob and Tom and their daughter Lottie. On 21st January 2003 the church received a Tyrone Crystal Vase from Roberta Moore, Seattle, U.S.A., in memory of her parents Mr. and Mrs. Robert Moore. The McClure family presented two hand-crafted wooden chairs for the vestibule in memory of their parents, Mr. and Mrs. R.J. McClure and in 2007 a similar wooden bench was presented for the vestibule in memory of Mr. Alan Kirk. It was the gift of his mother and father, Annie and Joseph Kirk and his sister Sandra. The new Irish Presbyterian Hymnbook was launched on 13th March 2005 and copies for the choir were presented in memory of Mr. J. Adam McClure, who had been a member of the choir for many years. The hymn supplement "Words of Worship" was revised and enlarged in June 2003.

PRESENTATIONS

Miss Anne McC. Kirkpatrick Lisboy, was honoured in 2005 at a ceremony in Church House, Fisherwick Place, Belfast, for her devoted service to the Presbyterian Orphan Society. She had been a collector for the society in the congregation for

Presentation to Mr. and Mrs. Arnold McClure in 2001 when they retired after twenty-one years as Freewill Offering secretaries. With them are Mr. Robert Patterson, treasurer, the Rev. Noel McClean, minister and Mr. Maurice Christie, secretary

Miss Anne McC. Kirkpatrick is presented with a Bible by the Rev. Noel McClean in gratitude for over fifty years of devoted service as a collector for the Presbyterian Orphan Society

over fifty years and still continues her collections with energy and enthusiasm. Mr. and Mrs. Arnold McClure were made a presentation in 2001 when they retired from their work as secretaries of the Freewill Offering after twenty-one years of service. Mr. and Mrs. Desmond Nevin were appointed to succeed them.

THREE MISSIONS

The Spiritual welfare of the congregation has not been forgotten during the ministry of the Rev. Noel McClean. Three missions have been held. The Very Rev. Dr. Andrew R. Rodgers, Dungannon, conducted a mission from Sunday 10th to Sunday 17th April 2002. The Rev. Dr. Cecil Grant, Mosside and Toberdoney, was the preacher at a mission during Easter Week, 2005 and a mission was included as part of the activities of the 350th year. It took place from Sunday 26th September to Sunday 3rd October 2010 and the preacher was the Rev. Albert Baxter, First Portglenone.

LIGNITE

At a meeting of committee on 24th June 2003…..

> "Mr. Thompson Elliott expressed thanks to Mr. Bob Richmond, on behalf of the committee, for all Bob's work and time spent in supporting the 'No To Lignite' campaign. This was seconded by Mr. William Moore. Mr. Richmond replied briefly and noted that further support would be necessary before the campaign was finished.'[14]

"Just Say No to Rural Destruction and to Lignite Mining" was a slogan which became well known across the Ballymoney area. It arose because of a plan launched in early 2003 by an Australian company to proceed with an open-cast lignite mine and a 600 megawatt power station in the local countryside. An area of about 5,000 acres was to be involved, including the homes and farm land of many members of First Kilraughts. The Manse itself and manse farm were in the very heart of the proposed lignite area. Mr. Bob Richmond was the chairman of COLD, an organization set up by local people and called the Collective Objectors to Lignite Development. Huge numbers of people attended protest meetings in Roseyards and Bushvale Church Halls and eventually the proposal was shelved. However, no one knows when it will re-appear but the people of First Kilraughts and neighbouring areas remain strongly committed to oppose the development of lignite as an energy source.

KATHRYN McCLEAN IN UGANDA

The Rev. Noel and Mrs. McClean's eldest daughter, Kathryn, went to Uganda in 2008 to work with the Africa Inland Mission on a project called Dwelling Places. She worked as a teacher and found the whole experience challenging but very rewarding.

She kept close contact with First Kilraughts throughout her year and in one of her letters she wrote:

> "Please pray for all the kids who are growing up on the streets of Kampingisa as their home. Pray for God's protection on them as the streets are horrible places and the children often get beatings from passers by and the police."[15]

She said:

> "Dwelling Places have given so much hope to over five hundred children over the past seven years and taken so many children out of hopeless situations."[16]

As the Visitation of Presbytery of 2009 put it:

> "Kathryn's work, serving in Uganda, has given the congregation's interest in mission a new dimension and impetus."[17]

MISS ANNA MARY McCLURE'S 100th BIRTHDAY

The Rt. Rev. Dr. J. Stafford Carson, Moderator of the General Assembly and the Rev. Noel McClean join Miss Anna Mary McClure for her one hundredth birthday celebrations, 9th January, 2010

On Saturday, 9th January 2010 Miss Anna Mary McClure celebrated her one hundredth birthday. She was joined by family and friends for the event and the attendance also included the Moderator of the General Assembly, the Rt. Rev. Dr. J. Stafford and Mrs. Carson and the Rev. Noel and Mrs. McClean. Miss McClure received the customary greeting from H.M. the Queen and First Kilraughts congregation sent a bouquet to her, the only centenarian in the recent history of the congregation and perhaps in the entire history of First Kilraughts.

Miss McClure was the daughter of Robert John and Margaret McClure of Ballynagashel. She was born on January 10th, 1910, and educated at Ballynagashel Primary School. She worshipped at First Kilraughts along with other members of her family, sitting in Pew 27 in the old church. Miss McClure worked on the family farm before taking up nursing as a career in 1938, receiving her training at Bethlem Royal Hospital, Kent. She was engaged in various spheres of nursing and held the position of

Deputy Matron in Chapel Allerton Hospital in Leeds until her retirement in 1975.

Miss McClure, at her hundredth birthday, recalled the values instilled in her by her parents, especially the need to attend worship, respect for others and the observance of the Lord's Day. A life long involvement in the church, which included service as a church elder, was coupled with charity work and, while in England, Miss McClure met Queen Mary in connection with her association with St. John Ambulance. Ill health prompted Miss McClure to return to the Ballymoney area in October 2001. She initially stayed in the Court Nursing Home but then transferred to Kirkhill Manor which she enjoyed very much, often speaking of it as "a home from home". She had a very high regard for its owner, Naomi Beggs, who cared for her so well and organised her one hundredth birthday celebrations.

The Rev. Noel McClean, speaking to the press at the event said:

> "Miss McClure is a most faithful example to us all in First Kilraughts. She attends worship regularly and has a most positive attitude to life."[18]

Mr. McClean also noted that she was a lady of considerable determination, anxious to keep as much of her independence as possible and he recalled that she enjoyed driving until she was 91, in her cherished Morris Minor car, which she purchased when new.

Miss McClure died at Kirkhill Manor on 11th May 2010 and was buried in First Kilraughts Churchyard after a service in the church. She was survived by her brother John and a number of nieces and nephews.

CELEBRATIONS

On 21st September 2005 a large congregational gathering took place to celebrate the 30th anniversary of the opening of the church buildings. "1ˢᵗ K Kirk News" recorded it like this:

> "A large attendance of people of all ages gathered in the Robinson Hall for an evening of looking back and looking forward. The idea that inspired the event was the rebuilding of the Church after the disastrous fire on 4th April 1971 and the subsequent opening of the present building on 31ˢᵗ May 1975. We had opportunity in praise to thank God for the past and pray for His help for the future. The slide presentation by Alex Blair, our notable historian, kindled memories for many of our older members and educated many of our younger ones. Humorous recitations were given by Helen McQuiston. Musical items included the rendering of 'For the beauty of the earth' as well as solos on the harp. A real highlight of the evening was to learn from Claire, Jonathan and Kathryn of their experiences as they gave part of their summer to serve as short term missionaries in South Africa, Peru and Uganda respectively. Rev. McClean reminded the gathering that the church is always moving on and appropriately the motto of Presbyterianism is Ardens Sed Virens – Burning but living"[19]

The 350th year has been celebrated in a variety of events in 2010, some already mentioned and some which will be mentioned in Chapter 7.

A highlight was the Flower Festival held from Friday 21ˢᵗ to Sunday 23ʳᵈ May and featuring some dramatic floral arrangements under the direction of Mr. James Burnside. The Theme was "Let's Celebrate" and this was interpreted in fifteen artistic floral pieces each based on a text from the Bible. Large crowds, in splendid sunshine, enjoyed what was an outstanding and very beautiful part of the 350th Celebrations.

Other celebrations included a Family Fun Night organised

*Left: Mrs. Inez Richmond with Mrs. Sarah Brown at the floral display
"Let's Celebrate – Our Lord's Reign," which was in memory of Mr. Andrew
Brown, at the Flower Festival, 21st – 23rd May, 2010. Right: Flower Festival
display "Let's Celebrate – Our Shepherd,"*

*Mrs. Lorna McClure (left) and Miss Lilian Elliott beside the "Let's Celebrate
– In Praise" item at the Flower Festival, 21st – 23rd May, 2010*

by the Sunday School on 12th June, a Holiday Bible Club in the second week in August, a congregational meal held in the Robinson Hall on 15th September, a week of mission at the end of September, already mentioned, and a Children's Mission Weekend with Stephen Chambers from Friday 8th to Sunday 10th October. There was a visit from the former Minister, the Rev. David Thompson and his wife Angela on Sunday 12th September and the celebrations ended with the launch of this book on Thursday 18th November. On that evening the Presbyterian Historical Society of Ireland visited First Kilraughts and the present author gave a lecture on the history of the congregation.

VISITATION OF PRESBYTERY, 2009

A comprehensive picture of congregational life may be gleaned from the Finding of the Visitation of the Route Presbytery to First Kilraughts in 2009.

Presbytery paid tribute to the Rev. Noel McClean, speaking of his faithfulness, diligence and enthusiasm and noted:

> "While being aware of the history and traditions associated with this congregation, Mr. McClean also recognises that the Church must always be relevant to the needs of the people in the present and, in faith, look to God for His help in the future."[20]

With regard to the congregation in general, the Finding was equally positive:

> "The statistical returns for the congregation paint a very stable picture with regard to families. It is good to see that some new families have recently joined the congregation, and that all visitors receive a warm welcome. Together the minister and elders seek to encourage the members of the congregation in their service for our Lord Jesus."[21]

The Finding described First Kilraughts as "a busy congregation" with many different activities to cater for all age groups and spoke of the "excellent set of buildings" available in which to do this. The Finding concluded:

> "The Presbytery is impressed by the work done in First Kilraughts and congratulates all who give time and talents to the running of the church."[22]

THE FUTURE

It is therefore with confidence and hope that First Kilraughts contemplates the future. As the Finding of the Visitation said, it is a busy place. As well as all the organisations, the work of which will be outlined in Chapter 7, there are many efforts which take place at special times – for example Operation Christmas Child when members fill large numbers of shoe boxes with Christmas gifts for children in Eastern Europe and father afield. There is the tape ministry, organized by Mr. and Mrs. Jim Murray, which brings the service to those unable to be present at worship, and many give of their time in the practical running and upkeep of the church and its environs Mr. and Mrs. Robert Patterson have given outstanding service in this respect for many years and Mrs. Annie Brown looks after the cleaning of the church building. Grass cutting was done for many years by Mr. Joseph Guthrie and he was succeeded by Mr. Billy McKelvey. A group of people turn up when required to keep the graveyard tidy and many others, in their own special ways, contribute help as the need arises. There is a good spirit among the people and they are willing and anxious to offer their talents and expertise when required. So First Kilraughts goes forward, resting on the promise, put so confidently by the Psalmist:

> "But unto them that do Him fear
> God's mercy never ends;
> And to their children's children still
> His righteousness extends."[23]

Chapter 5

Notes and Reference

1. "The Chronicle", 26th April 1997.
2. "Reach Out", June – July 2008, p.8.
3. Minute of Meeting of Kirk Session, 19th January 1998.
4. Minute of Meeting of Kirk Session, 7th March 1999.
5. See Kirk Session Minute, 14th June, 1999.
6. Finding of Visitation by Presbytery of Route to First Kilraughts, Sept. 1999.
7. Ibid.
8. Ibid.
9. See Letter included in Session Minute Book (1984-2001) p. 280.
10. "Ballymoney Times", 16th August 2000.
11. Ibid.
12. Ibid.
13. See Letter included in Session Minute Book (1984-2001) p. 281.
14. Minute of Meeting of Committee, 24th June 2003.
15. See "1st K Kirk News", Vol. 8, December 2008.
16. Ibid.
17. Finding of Visitation by Presbytery of Route to First Kilraughts, 2009.
18. "Ballymoney Times", 13th January 2010.
19. See "1st K. Kirk News", Vol 5, p19.
20. Finding of Visitation of Route Presbytery to First Kilraughts, 2009.
21. Ibid.
22. Ibid.
23. Metrical Psalm 103, v.17.

Chapter 6

KIRK SESSION and COMMITTEE

THE KIRK SESSION

The Kirk Session consists of members of the congregation, elected by their fellow members, who, with the minister, have spiritual oversight of the people.   Mr. Justice R.D. Megaw described the elders of his youth in First Kilraughts as "a sedate company".   This chapter looks at those in the eldership over a hundred years later and if "sedate" might not be the most obvious adjective to use with regard to them, they have still maintained an important leadership role in the life of First Kilraughts.

When the story of this book begins in 1971 First Kilraughts Kirk Session had twelve elders.   They were:

> William Carson, Artiferral and later Ballycastle,
>   ordained 12th April 1947.

> Robert Robinson, Drumavaddy,
>   ordained 12th April 1947.

> William Gamble, Ganaby,
>   ordained 28th October 1951.

> W. Arthur Tweed, Glennylough,
>   ordained 28th October 1951.

> Thomas Tweed, The Mullan, Magheraboy Upper,
>   ordained 28th October 1951.

> Thomas L. Boyd, Lissanoure, Loughgiel,
>   ordained 24th May 1959.

> Andrew McR. Brown, B.Agr., Carnageeragh,
>   ordained 24th May 1959.

> James Dobbin, Kilraughts,
>   ordained 24th May 1959.

William Kirkpatrick, Ballytaggart,
    ordained 24th May 1959.

Thomas Lamont, Calhame,
    ordained 24th May 1959.

Robert James McClure, Ballynagashel,
    ordained 24th May 1959.

James Robinson, Ballynaloob,
    Co-opted from Ballyfrenis Kirk Session,
    May 1963.

The Rev. F.A. Robinson with the Kirk Session in 1960. Front row (left to right): Messrs. Robert Robinson, John Hanna, Robert Holmes, James Patterson, William Gamble, Robert James McClure. Back row: Messrs. W. Arthur Tweed, Austin A Sayers, William Kirkpatrick, William Carson, Thomas Lamont, James Dobbin, Thomas Tweed, Andrew McR. Brown and Thomas L. Boyd.
When Mr. Bell was installed the Kirk Session consisted of eleven of these men with Mr. James Robinson, co-opted 1963. The eleven were: Messrs. R. Robinson, W. Gamble, R.J. McClure, W.A. Tweed, W. Kirkpatrick, W. Carson, T. Lamont, J. Dobbin, T. Tweed, A. McR. Brown and T.L. Boyd

Mr. Robinson had been Clerk of Session from June 1964.

Four of these elders did not live to see the new church opened and dedicated. They were William Gamble, Thomas Tweed, James Dobbin and James Robinson. Three died within a few months of each other in 1973.

MR. JAMES DOBBIN

James Dobbin died on 14th February 1973 and his death was recorded in the Session Minute Book as "a grievous loss." Mr. Dobbin's first wife was Miss Elizabeth Henry, and it was due to their marriage that Mr. Dobbin joined First Kilraughts Church. He came to live at the Henry farm at Kilraughts and was soon identified with the work of the congregation. For two lengthy periods he served with great devotion as sexton or church officer; he was the grave digger for many years and he also played a big part in the life of the community. As the local pig butcher, he went round the farms of Kilraughts showing his skill and providing a very important and useful service. He was also insurance agent for the area and, when there were few cars in the countryside, he put his at the disposal of his neighbours when they had to undertake long journeys. A most helpful, amiable and pleasant person, he suffered the loss of his first wife at an early age. His second wife, Miss Mary Taylor from Bushmills, gave him the same strong support in all his work as his first wife had done. They were greatly devoted to First Kilraughts Church and visitors were always sure of a gracious welcome, with Mr. Dobbin taking care to show them to a pew.

It was Mr. Dobbin who discovered the fire on Sunday, 4th April 1971. He arrived in the early morning to put on the heat and get the church ready for the service. He recalled, as he entered the building, he saw a huge flash of light passing across the ceiling and in a few minutes the whole place was in flames. No-one was more upset by this tragedy than Mr. Dobbin, for he loved the place. As congregational activities increased, he was there virtually every night and it would have been impossible to adequately pay him for the many hours he gave to the care of the buildings.

It was therefore appropriate that on the night before his funeral – the night of Thursday 15th February 1972 – his body rested in the church hall. He had been an elder for nearly thirteen years, but his service to the congregation spanned half a century.

MR JAMES ROBINSON

The Clerk of Session, Mr. James Robinson, died on 27th April 1973. With his wife and family, Mr. Robinson had come to reside at Ballynaloob. He joined First Kilraughts congregation in May 1963 on certificate from Ballyfrenis church. He had been a member of Kirk Session there and became the first elder ever to be co-opted to First Kilraughts Session. In June 1964 he was appointed Clerk in succession to Mr. James Patterson, Drumabest, who had died on 21st July 1963. The position had remained vacant for nearly a year.

Mr. Robinson was an officer in the Department of Agriculture and was highly esteemed by the farmers of the local area. At his funeral service, the Rev. Robin Bell outlined his career in agriculture and paid tribute to his work in First Kilraughts. He said:

> "As Session Clerk, James Robinson took an intense interest in the people of the congregation and their welfare. On many occasions, he showed his fine qualities as a man and a leader, although his influence was always exercised quietly and without fuss."[1]

The Session's Memorial Minute gave highest praise to Mr. Robinson's

> "…outstanding services as elder and Clerk of Session and to his great personal qualities and fine example of Christian living."[2]

MR. THOMAS TWEED

Mr. Thomas Tweed, The Mullan, Magheraboy Upper, died on Tuesday, 1st May 1973.

The Tweeds were among the first Planter families to arrive in Kilraughts from Scotland early in the seventeenth century and, through the generations, they have been members of the congregation. A life-long member, Mr. Thomas Tweed farmed the old home farm at The Mullan and was well-known in the farming community.

In his early years he had been involved in the Afternoon Sunday School which met in Ballymacwilliam School and later became a teacher in Craigatempin Sunday School. For many years he taught a class of senior boys there and was Superintendent from 1955 to 1972. He was ordained an elder on 28th October 1951 and gave faithful service for the next twenty-two years.

A man of great friendship and warmth of personality, he enjoyed meeting people and conversing with them. He delighted in welcoming visitors to First Kilraughts and ensuring they felt at home in the congregation.

MR. WILLIAM GAMBLE

Mr. William Gamble came from Garryduff, married Miss Jeannie Holmes, Ganaby, and thus joined First Kilraughts congregation. He was manager of Moffett's bicycle and hardware business in Main Street, Ballymoney, and respected in the business life of the town.

A deeply religious man, with a dignified and gentle personality, he was an esteemed elder for just over twenty-three years. He was the Superintendent of Ganaby Afternoon Sunday School until it closed in 1969, having succeeded his father-in-law, Mr. Robert Holmes, in the position.

First Kilraughts Kirk Session placed on record its gratitude to him and conveyed their sympathy to his daughter, Miss Marjorie C. Gamble, B.A. at the time of his death on 21st November 1974. He was aged 81 years and the Session's tribute spoke of his "many fine Christian characteristics" and the commitment he had shown to Christ throughout his long life.

In her reply to the Session's letter, Miss Gamble said:

> "Although my father felt unable, in recent months, to play as full a part in the affairs of the Session as formerly, he was always interested in what was happening and prayed constantly for God's blessing within the life of the Church".[3]

NEW CLERK AND NEW ELDERS

The deaths of these four members depleted the Session considerably, especially at a time when the spiritual welfare of the people was so important in the challenging days of the erection of the new church.

A successor to Mr. James Robinson as Clerk of Session was a priority and, at a meeting of Kirk Session on 25th May 1973, Mr. Andrew McR. Brown, B. Agr., was elected. New elders were also needed but their election was delayed until after the new church was opened and congregational life had returned to some semblance of normality.

Elections were held in 1976 and eight new elders were ordained at a special evening service on Sunday, 28th March. The new elders were;

Samuel Alexander Blair

Thompson Elliott

Robert Moore Kirkpatrick

Robert James Arnold McClure

James McIlhatton

William McIlhatton Moore

Robert Patterson

James Richmond

The local newspapers carried this report of the Ordination Service:

> "The church was filled with a large congregation for the occasion and the elders-elect entered in procession, preceded by the two senior elders of the congregation, Mr. Robert Robinson and Mr. William Carson, and followed by the existing Kirk Session, the Commission of the Presbytery of Route and the officiating ministers.
>
> The Moderator of the Route Presbytery, the Rev. H.W. Brooks, Armoy, presided, and the sermon was preached by the senior minister of First Kilraughts, the Rev. F.A. Robinson. The Clerk of Presbytery, the Rev. J.G. Leitch, read the Rule of Faith, after which the Moderator put the prescribed questions to the elders-elect. They then signed the General Assembly's Formula of Subscription to the Westminster Confession of Faith, after which they were solemnly ordained and installed to office by the Moderator with the laying on of hands, the other presbyters assisting. After the Right Hand of Fellowship had been extended to the new elders, an impressive charge was delivered by the Rev. George E. Cromey, Ballyweaney, Moderator of the Synod of Ballymena and Coleraine. Also taking part in the service was the minister of First Kilraughts, the Rev. Robert McC. Bell.
>
> Afterwards, the wives of the existing Kirk Session and ladies of the congregation entertained the new elders and their families and friends to supper in the church hall."[4]

The membership of Kirk Session was thus increased to sixteen but soon one elder resigned on moving to Ballycastle. He was Mr. Thomas L. Boyd, Lissanoure, Loughgiel. Mr. Boyd had joined the congregation when he became farm manager for James Mackie & Sons of Belfast at their estate at Lisanoure Castle. In the years after the Second World War he built up the estate and had a fine herd of Ayrshire cattle which produced milk, supplied to Ballycastle boarding houses in the summer and to Nestles for processing in the winter. Much respected, he had decided to retire to Ballycastle and a Bible was presented to him as a farewell gift from the Session at a meeting on Sunday, 29th July 1979.

MR ROBERT ROBINSON

One of the congregation's Senior Elders died on 13th July 1984. He was Mr. Robert Robinson, Drumavaddy, Culcrum. Mr. Robinson had been an elder for thirty-seven years and he was eighty-seven years of age.

A farmer, Orangeman and teacher in Knockahollet Sunday School, Mr. Robinson gave dedicated service to First Kilraughts Church and the local community.

Speaking at his funeral service the Rev. R. McC Bell took as his text the verse from Ecclesiastes chapter 9:

"The righteous… are in the hand of God."

Mr. Bell said Mr. Robinson was a man of deep Christian faith and a good neighbour, who would be sadly missed in the home and community.[5-]

NEW CLERK OF SESSION

In a letter dated 5th June 1985 Mr. Andrew McR Brown, B.Agr., stated that he wished to relinquish the position of Clerk of Session. This was accepted "with regret" and Session then proceeded to elect a new clerk. At a meeting on 12th June 1985

Mr. James McIlhatton was elected Clerk but he asked for a few days to consider the office and this resulted in his decision not to accept it.[6] A further meeting was held on 30th July 1985 when Mr. S. Alex Blair, M.A., was elected.

However, as the minute of the meeting recorded:

> "Mr. Blair thanked the members for their confidence in him and, after stating certain hesitations which were in his mind as to his availability at all times to carry out the duties, he agreed to accept the appointment."[7]

In 1986 two elders died – Mr. Thomas Lamont in July and Dr. R. Moore Kirkpatrick in December.

MR. THOMAS LAMONT

Mr. Thomas Lamont, 9 Glenlough Road, died in the Route Hospital, Ballymoney, on 29th July 1986. He was a life-long member of the congregation and had been an elder for twenty-seven years. He was the congregation's representative elder at the time of his death and had been a member of the church choir and taught in the Morning Sunday School.

A Memorial Minute passed by Kirk Session included the following:

> "Mr. Lamont will be particularly remembered for the attachment he had to Craigatempin Hall and all that was done there. For a great number of years he taught a class in the Afternoon Sunday School held there and later became Superintendent. He was the leader of the Craigatempin Prayer Union and a Trustee of the Hall. Especially interested in evangelical outreach, Mr. Lamont was a strong supporter of both the Faith Mission and the Christian Workers' Union.
>
> For a period he also served as Superintendent of the Afternoon Sunday School at Lavin, which prospered under his leadership.

Although in indifferent health for the last number of years, Mr. Lamont was described by his doctor as a "model patient" and faced illness in a Christian spirit with courage and hope. The attendance at his funeral indicated the wide impact he made on our community."[8]

DR. R. MOORE KIRKPATRICK

The death of Dr. R. Moore Kirkpatrick, Lavin House, Knockahollet, on 3rd December 1986, caused widespread sorrow throughout North Antrim.

In a Memorial Minute, the Kirk Session recorded:

"...their gratitude to God for one who, in his life and work gave to the utmost of his strength and skill in the service of others."[9]

The Minute continued:

"Within the medical profession he earned the respect and esteem of his fellow practitioners. As a doctor he worked long and hard, not sparing himself, always available when called, meticulous in his attention to detail, and very often visiting his patients early and late to give them all possible assistance. His devotion to his patients took a tremendous toll on his time and energy, yet at no time during his thirty-six years in practice at Lavin did he ease up in the work of healing, to which he devoted himself entirely.

When he retired in 1976 he had the opportunity to spend time with his family and pursue his many hobbies and interests. We thank God that he was enabled to enjoy the blessings and fellowship of those ten years of retirement.

Dr. Moore Kirkpatrick loved God and had a deep Christian faith. He was a deeply devout and generous member of First Kilraughts. Indeed it was fitting that his retirement from professional duties should coincide with his taking up the duties of Ruling Elder in this congregation. He was ordained to the eldership on 28th March 1976 and always took a keen interest in the welfare of the people of his district. At meetings of Session and Committee he was listened to with respect at all times, and we remember he was present with us at our last meeting and, as always, in his own quiet way, contributed words of encouragement and wisdom. He officiated at the November Communion, being present at all the services of that Communion Season, and was in church with us the Sunday previous to his death.

The members of our neighbouring congregation of Bushvale, with which his family has many connections have, like us, lost a very great friend who showed a keen interest in their welfare.

Dr. Kirkpatrick was a highly-respected member of the Masonic Order in which he attained a very senior rank. He was also a keen member of Ballymoney Probus Club during his years of retirement. He loved good music, enjoyed travel, read widely, and had a special love for his home, his family and his garden.

In every aspect of his life Moore Kirkpatrick was one in whom sheer goodness abounded. In Kilraughts we remember his gentleness and humility, and the warmth of his friendship. We all admired the courage and faith with which he met the onset of illness two years ago and the whole community is bereaved by his death."[10]

Dr. Kirkpatrick's funeral service was held in the church and he was buried in Kilraughts Old Graveyard. His widow, Dr. Marjory Kirkpatrick, later wrote to the Kirk Session thanking them for their part in her husband's funeral service. She paid tribute to "how efficiently and graciously" they ushered and greeted "all our friends" and continued:

> "It was all done with great dignity and feeling and he would have been so proud of Kilraughts – the church he loved."[11]

The congregation suffered another sad loss when the former congregational secretary, Mr. W. Arthur Tweed, died suddenly on Wednesday, 30th March 1988.

MR W. ARTHUR TWEED

Mr. William Arthur Tweed, "The Glen", 88 Frosses Road, had been an elder for nearly thirty-seven years. The Kirk Session's Memorial Minute placed ....

> "...On record their gratitude to God for a life so full and so devoted to the work of the church. He passed away within the church buildings, whose care was his constant concern for so many years and where he spent so many happy hours. It was while enjoying his favourite recreation, a game of bowls, that his Home-Call suddenly came and the swiftness with which he was taken has left us all shocked and deeply saddened."[12]

The Minute continued

> "William Arthur Tweed was brought up in the congregation and his outstanding gifts of heart and mind marked him out as a key figure in the church he loved. He was elected to the Congregational Committee in 1938, becoming its Secretary in 1951, which office he held with distinction until 1987 when he retired. He was the last survivor of the six men ordained to the Ruling Eldership on 28th October, 1951, and at all times he played a full part in the work of Kirk Session, particularly at the Communion Season. Very popular in the homes of his district, he was most regular in

his attendance at meetings of Session and was always ready to give us the benefit of his opinion on matters being discussed.

However, it was his integrity and faithfulness, energy and efficiency as Congregational Secretary which made the greatest impact on First Kilraughts. Heavy demands were made upon him, especially after the destruction of the church building by fire in April 1971 and throughout the period of building the new church. Mr. Tweed never flagged under the heavy work-load imposed and when he retired in 1987 he said he was thankful to have been spared to see the new church dedicated, paid for in full, and the congregation in a sound financial position. Twice he was honoured with tangible tokens of appreciation for his services as Congregational Secretary.

In the wider community, Mr. Tweed was a trustee of Craigatempin Hall and a member of the Ulster Farmers' Union.

As a young man he spent a short time in the United States of America and was one of the first group of students admitted to Greenmount Agricultural College. As an agricultural officer, he served in South Armagh, where he met his wife, the former Miss Muriel Simms, Mountnorris.

On their marriage, they made their home at the Tweed family farm, "The Glen", and there their family was born. To Mrs. Tweed and to Margaret, Elizabeth, Barbara, Audrey and Samuel, as well as to Mr. Tweed's sisters, Marion, Julia and Lil, the Session extends its deepest sympathy and offers prayers for their support and comfort in their time of such sudden sorrow and loss."[13]

NEW ELDERS ORDAINED 1989

The Kirk Session was augmented by the election of five new elders in 1989. They were:

Joseph Lamont

John McCarroll Tweed McClure

Robert McLernon Richmond

John Alexander Graham Robinson

Samuel Moore Tweed

They were ordained at a special evening service on Sunday, 22nd October 1989. The newspaper reports gave the details:

"A Commission of the Route Presbytery carried out

Ordination of Elders, 22nd October, 1989
The new elders are seated with the Moderator of the Route Presbytery, the Rev. Doug. R. Baker. They are (left to right): Messrs. J.A. Graham Robinson, Carl McClure, Joseph Lamont, Samuel M. Tweed and Robert McL. Richmond. Standing, at the back, is the Commission of the Presbytery: Mr. Wm. Logan, the Rev. Maurice Barr, the Rev. Robin Bell, the Rev. W.J. Watson, the Rev. H.B. Wallace, Mr. Joseph Patton CBE and Mr. Robert Wasson

the ceremony, with the Moderator, the Rev. Doug. R. Baker, Corrymeela, presiding. The Clerk of Session of First Kilraughts, Mr. S. Alex. Blair, welcomed the Commission and the visitors, and an appropriate sermon on "The Church" was preached by the Rev. Maurice Barr, Ballyweaney. The Clerk of Presbytery, the Rev. H. Barkley Wallace, Bushmills, read the Rule of Faith and the Act of Ordination and Installation was carried out by the Moderator, assisted by the Clerk and the Rev. W.J. Watson, Roseyards.

The Rev. Robert McC. Bell, minister of the First Kilraughts congregation, also took part and the choir, with Mr. Maurice Christie at the organ, sang the anthem 'How Sweet the Name'. An eloquent charge to the newly-ordained elders was given by Mr. Wallace and the offering was for the Students' Bursary Fund.

Afterwards, at a reception in the Church Hall, Mr. Bell welcomed the new elders to the Kirk Session. He said he knew they would make a useful contribution to the deliberations of Session and give leadership in the congregation and service to their church.

Speeches of congratulations to the new elders were made by the Moderator of Presbytery as well as by the Rev. F.A. Robinson, senior minister of First Kilraughts, who said he had baptised four of them. Mr. Robinson said he could look back on almost sixty years in First Kilraughts and that he had greatly enjoyed that evening's service. He also thanked the ladies of the congregation for the supper which they had served.

Mr. J.A. Graham Robinson, on behalf of the new elders, replied to the greetings and good wishes which had been expressed and thanked everyone for their encouragement and support."[14]

MR. WILLIAM CARSON, J.P.

First Kilraughts Session lost its Senior Elder in the death on 22nd May 1995 of Mr. William Carson, Redwoods, 14 Drumavoley Road, Ballycastle, and formerly of Artiferral. He had been an elder for forty-eight years and was aged ninety-seven. Mr. Carson gave a lifetime of service to First Kilraughts Church.

As a young man in his twenties he was elected to the congregational committee and from 1932 to 1954 he served as church treasurer, bringing his shrewd and balanced judgement to that very responsible position. He was ordained a ruling elder on 12th April 1947, during the ministry of the Rev. F.A. Robinson, with whom he enjoyed the happiest of friendships for sixty-four years.

In the life of the wider community Mr. Carson represented the Kilraughts district on Ballymoney Rural District Council for many years. The owner of a large farming enterprise at Artiferral, which Mr. Carson inherited from his father and where his family had farmed for generations, he was always in the forefront of agricultural progress and his farm was often visited as a show-piece of the best in agricultural development of the day. As a young man he had a thirst for knowledge and became a member of the Book Club at Ballymacwillian School, where he had his first experience of discussion and debates on learned matters. His enjoyment of literature and cultural activities remained with him throughout his long life and he loved reading and regularly attended many cultural events. Another of his favourite recreations was sport, especially bowls and golf and he was one of the first farmers in North Antrim to set aside some time on a regular basis for a round of golf, as a break from his farming routine.

His special love was nature – birds, flowers, shrubs and especially trees. They were his friends and had personality as far as he was concerned. His beautiful garden, full of trees and shrubs, which he planted at the house which he had built for his retirement, Redwoods, Drumavoley Road, Ballycastle, gave him ample scope for this hobby and he enjoyed working amongst his trees and showing them to his many visitors.

As the years passed he had the sadness of bereavement by the death of his wife Margaret in December 1980. His loneliness was greatly relieved not long afterwards when his sister Josephine moved from Portstewart to live with him. She remained with him until his death and attended his funeral service in First Kilraughts in her one hundredth year. In the last years of his life Mr. Carson was unable to attend church because of failing hearing and eye-sight, but he enjoyed the visits of his friends from Kilraughts who brought him news of the congregation. He was especially pleased always to see the minister, the Rev. Robin Bell, who regularly visited him and became a close friend.

The Memorial Minute of Kirk Session included the following tribute:

> "William Carson was a man of many talents and much ability, who served his church and community assiduously and with much dedication. However, he remained essentially a humble, quiet, retiring gentleman with an old-world courtesy and charm, which endeared him to all who were fortunate enough to know him as fellow-elder and friend. We give thanks to God for his long life of rich achievement, his witness to the eternal truths of the Gospel and his lifetime of service given so graciously to his church and community."[15]

MR ANDREW McR. BROWN, B.Agr.

The sudden death of Mr. Andrew McRoberts Brown, B.Agr., shocked the congregation and the entire community. He died on the afternoon of Sunday, 13th April 1997, just a short time after he had attended morning worship in First Kilraughts.

A native of the Saintfield area of Co. Down, Mr. Brown joined the congregation in 1956, not long after his marriage to the former Miss Sarah Killough, Carnageeragh. They established their home at Carnageeragh on the other side of the road from the Killough farmstead and there he lived for the rest of his life and there he died in his chair by the fireside.

A graduate in Agriculture of the Queen's University of Belfast, his first post as an official of the then Ministry of Agriculture was as Advisory Officer for North Antrim. Later he became Dairying Inspector for Co. Londonderry. Throughout his working career, Mr. Brown was an esteemed figure in the farming community, noted for his integrity, humanity and devotion to the farmers' interests. His father had been a founder of the Young Farmers' Clubs Movement and Andrew Brown gave strong support to Kilraughts Young Farmers' Club, in which he held the positions of president and patron. In First Kilraughts church he served faithfully as Secretary of Freewill Offering from 1957 to 1970, a teacher in the Morning Sunday School for many years, a member of the Bible Study Group and of the Bowling Club. He was ordained a Ruling Elder on 24th May 1959 and in May 1973 became Clerk of Session. He remained Clerk until his retirement in June 1985.

The Memorial Minute passed by the Kirk Session recalled his many achievements and continued...

> "His steady hand steered the congregation with assurance and vision through the exciting but often difficult days of building the new church and his interest in the church and its people was evident to all. He had a realistic and enthusiastic approach to the church's work and was always encouraging and supportive of all that was done. His ready smile, kindness of nature and wide sympathy made him a welcome visitor in the homes of the people. His balanced judgment, strength

of character and leadership qualities were recognised and valued by his fellow elders and the congregation as a whole, who held him in a position of respect and esteem."[16]

This minute was passed at the first meeting of Kirk Session in the ministry of the Rev. David H. Thompson, who had been installed in the congregation a few days after Mr. Brown's funeral. He inherited a Kirk Session which numbered fourteen in total, but soon this was reduced by the deaths of three elders during 1998 and 1999.

MR JAMES RICHMOND

Mr. James Richmond, Toberbilly, 196 Kilraughts Road, died on Saturday 21st February 1998 in Coleraine Hospital after a lengthy illness.

Born on 20th May 1920, Mr. Richmond spent his early years at Balleney, Armoy. As a young man, he came to Toberbilly to farm and joined First Kilraughts congregation. Later he became a member of committee and was ordained a Ruling Elder on 28th March 1976. He took a deep interest in many aspects of the church's work and was most supportive of everything being done. For relaxation, he enjoyed the happy atmosphere of the Bowling Club, where he spent many an enjoyable evening. As a farmer, Mr. Richmond showed much skill and enthusiasm. He was most industrious, winning the respect and esteem of the whole farming community. They recognised him as one who took a pride in his work and was always happy in his farmyard and his fields, which he maintained to very high standards.

The Session recorded:

> "We remember with gratitude his life of rich achievement, his kindly manner, his neighbourliness and his gift for friendship. Although he suffered a long illness, he felt well enough to be at church fairly

recently. He loved to worship in First Kilraughts and he did so with his wife and family every Sunday while his health permitted.

He was the centre of his home, a place which meant much to him and he greatly enjoyed his retirement home, which he had specially built for his wife and himself adjacent to the farm."[17]

NEW ELDERS ELECTED AND ORDAINED, 1999

The only ordination of elders which took place during the ministry of the Rev. David H. Thompson was held in the church on the evening of Sunday, 24th January 1999. Five new members of Kirk Session had been elected. They were:

Maurice Francis Robinson Christie

Joseph Kirk

David McMillan

Jim Murray

John Thompson Reid

The service was conducted by the Moderator of Presbytery, the Rev. J. Trevor Magowan, St. James's, Ballymoney. The scripture reading was by the senior minister of First Kilraughts, the Rev. R. McC. Bell, and the Clerk of Presbytery, the Rev. H. Barkley Wallace, Bushmills, read the Rule of Faith. The preacher was the Rev. Kenneth D. W. Crowe, Bushvale, who also gave the Charge. The prescribed questions were put by the Moderator, after which the new elders were ordained by the laying-on of hands, the Moderator leading in prayer. All present were welcomed to First Kilraughts by the minister, the Rev. D. H. Thompson, and supper followed in the Robinson Hall.

MR. J.A. GRAHAM ROBINSON, M.A., B.Ed.

The death of Mr. John Alexander Graham Robinson, M.A., B.Ed., on 11th March 1999 brought great sorrow to First

Kilraughts and to the entire Ballymoney and North Antrim area. He was only forty-seven years of age and had suffered a long illness, which he bore with great courage.

Brought up in the congregation of Balteagh in Co. Londonderry and educated at Limavady Grammar School and Stranmillis College, Belfast, Mr. Robinson was appointed to the teaching staff of Dalriada School, Ballymoney, in 1974. After his marriage to Miss Betty Kennedy and his appointment to Dalriada School, he came to live at 41 Ballyveely Road, Pharis, and joined First Kilraughts congregation.

Mr. Robinson soon won for himself a place in the hearts of the people and gave much of his time to the work of the congregation, teaching in the Morning Sunday School, working as an officer in the Boys' Brigade and taking a leadership role in the Youth Fellowship. Indeed, he was a strong supporter of everything to do with the life of the church. In 1979 he was elected to the Congregational Committee and on 2nd March 1987 became Congregational Secretary in succession to Mr. W. Arthur Tweed. On 22nd October 1989 Mr. Robinson was ordained as a Ruling Elder in First Kilraughts. He remained Congregational Secretary until January 1999 when he had to resign due to ill health. Some weeks later an inscribed Bible and a cheque were presented to him as a token of the congregation's gratitude for all his work on their behalf.

He became Head of Geography in Dalriada School and was highly regarded for his skill as a teacher and his approachable and caring nature. He was meticulous in everything he did and had tremendous enthusiasm and great qualities of endurance. As the Kirk Session Minute, passed at the time of his death, recorded:

> "When illness struck, Mr. Robinson showed determination and strength. His faith was never more real to him than in those last five years and life was

never sweeter nor more challenging. He often said they were his best years and the manner in which he faced them was an example of Christian faith and courage to us all.

Session places on record its gratitude to God for Graham Robinson, his example, his faith, his assurance and his vision. We recall that he was an academic of standing with a higher degree from the Open University, a teacher of great patience and thoroughness, but we remember him especially for his love of his church and of its Head, his Saviour, Jesus Christ. We give thanks to God for all that Graham Robinson was able to do by word, act and example here in First Kilraughts and we offer prayers for their comfort to his wife and family, who meant so much to him and of whom he was, so rightly, extremely proud."[18]

MR. WILLIAM KIRKPATRICK

The death of Mr. William Kirkpatrick on 25th June 1999 at Knockans Lodge, Finvoy, removed from the congregation its oldest member and an elder who had been forty years in office.

William Kirkpatrick spent his entire working life on the family farm at Ballytaggart and was well-known for his industry and the quality of his farming. He loved the land and this gave him deep roots in a place where his family had farmed for generations. He was keenly interested in the life of the countryside, its history, its personalities, and he had a clear and retentive memory which enabled him to recall incidents and events easily and vividly.

A gifted conversationalist and of a very friendly disposition, Mr. Kirkpatrick believed in the country virtue of good neighbourliness and he and his car were at the disposal of many. He did many good turns for many people and was never happier than when he was helping others.

A life-long member of First Kilraughts congregation, he attended church every Sunday, while health permitted, and even in his nineties came regularly and always made a special point of being present at Communion. The church was the centre of his interest and a very special place as far as he was concerned. He was very sad when the old church was burned but so happy when the new building was completed and opened. Mr. Kirkpatrick was first elected to the congregational committee in 1947 and on 24th May 1959 he was ordained a ruling elder. He held that position for over 40 years and, although unable to act in the last few years, while he was in good health he faithfully attended to his duties as an elder, visiting in his district and carrying out all his work with dignity and dedication.

He had the great joy of travelling to the United Sates of America to visit his sister and many other Kilraughts folk there and this was one of the most memorable experiences of his long life.

He cared devotedly for his wife – the former Miss Margaret Morton – through a long illness and he, in turn, was cared for by his daughters and in his last years by the staff at Knockans Lodge Residential Home, Finvoy.

Kirk Session recorded their indebtedness to Mr. Kirkpatrick…

> "… for all his support and work with regard to First Kilraughts congregation and give thanks for his long life, which was one of great usefulness, lived to the glory of God and for His honour. We recall with gratitude his gentleness, his calm nature and his peace of mind, which enabled him to have an inner peace, which he retained to the end."[19]

VACANCY

In the vacancy which followed the departure of the Rev. David H. Thompson to Strand Church in Belfast, two elders resigned. Mr. James McIlhatton resigned on 8th October 2000 and the Clerk, Mr. S. Alex Blair, M.A., resigned at a special meeting of the Kirk Session held on 28th October 2000. Many of the congregation were shocked by these resignations, but Mr. Blair assured the Kirk Session on the night of his resignation that…

"…there was no foundation or cause for concern."[20]

Later, at a short meeting of Kirk Session held on Sunday 10th February 2002…

> "…It was proposed by the Clerk (Arnold McClure), seconded by Bob Richmond, that the Kirk Session should acknowledge the fifteen years that Mr. S.A. Blair had been clerk."[21]

Subsequently Mr. McClure and the new minister, the Rev. Noel McClean, called on Mr. Blair at his home and presented him with a substantial travel voucher as a token of the Session's gratitude for all his work.

NEW CLERK OF SESSION

A new Clerk was appointed at a meeting on 8th November 2000, presided over by the convener-in-charge of the vacancy the Rev. E.J. Hyndman, Roseyards. Mr. Arnold McClure was elected unanimously and, in accepting, he…

> "…thanked the members for bestowing this honour upon him and asked for their prayerful support. He said he would try to serve to the utmost of his ability."[22]

When the Rev. Noel McClean was installed as minister on 17th August 2001 there were 14 members of Kirk Session. They were:

Robert James McClure

Thompson Elliott

Robert James Arnold McClure

William McIlhatton Moore

Robert Patterson

Joseph Lamont

John McCarroll Tweed McClure

Robert McLernon Richmond

Samuel Moore Tweed

Maurice Francis Robinson Christie

Joseph Kirk

David McMullan

Jim Murray

John Thompson Reid

Two of these have since died – Mr. R.J. McClure and Mr. Thompson Elliott.

MR ROBERT JAMES McCLURE

Mr. Robert James McClure, 187 Kilraughts Road, died at Ratheane Private Nursing Home, Coleraine, on Friday, 11th November 2005. He was in his ninety-fourth year and had been an elder for forty-six years.

Mr. McClure spent his entire working life on the family farm at Ballynagashel and was a life-long member of First Kilraughts. A quiet man, Mr. McClure spoke little in the courts of the church but, when he spoke, he did so with understanding and his fellow elders knew he talked sense. Ever encouraging and with a down-to-earth approach, Mr. McClure was held in high esteem in First Kilraughts Church and in the Kilraughts Community.

The Memorial Minute passed at the time of his death also noted:

"As long as he was able, he attended services and meetings of the congregation and retained a keen interest in all the affairs of the church right to the end of his earthly life.

He was a member of the Bowling Club and, although taking up this hobby comparatively late in life, was a keen and very proficient bowler. He gave practical service to the church in any way that he could and is remembered as one of the last members of committee to attempt maintaining the graveyard with his scythe. Predeceased by his wife Lila (with whom he shared more than 60 years of marriage), he is remembered with affection by the congregation he loved and served."[23]

MR THOMPSON ELLIOTT

Another life-long member of the congregation and an elder for thirty-three years, Mr. Thompson Elliott died at the Robinson Memorial Hospital, Ballymoney, on Sunday 25th October 2009.

In the early years of his life Mr. Elliott worked for local farmers and in latter years for building contractors. He knew the value of work and always gave of his best to his employers.

The Memorial Minute passed by the Session included the following tribute:

"He was held in the very highest esteem by the congregation and most of all by the families of his district where he faithfully and diligently made his visitations until a few years ago when failing eyesight prevented him from so doing. Nevertheless, his disability did not deter him from his seat in the pew until a couple of weeks before his death."[24]

The Minute concluded:

"Thompson's faith was well founded in his Lord and Saviour Jesus Christ and this was borne out when he bore with great fortitude the loss of his eldest son Lewis in a tragic accident in 1999 and the loss of his wife Mary in 2000. The Kirk Session will remember him for his wise counsel, kindness and the gentlemanly manner he portrayed to all with whom he came into contact."[25]

The Kirk Session, 2010.
Seated (left to right); Messrs. Wm. Moore, Arnold McClure (Clerk), the Rev. Noel McClean, Messrs. Robert Patterson, Joseph Lamont, Standing: Messrs. Robert Richmond, David McMillan, Joseph Kirk, Maurice Christie, Jim Murray, John Reid, Samuel Tweed and Carl McClure

THE 350th YEAR

In the 350th year Kilraughts Kirk Session continues to remain vigilant with regard to the spiritual affairs of the congregation. Elders visit in their districts, distribute communion tokens and arrange their participatory roles in the twice-yearly communion services. They meet regularly and deal with whatever matters come within their remit. Recently they have discussed parental guidelines for baptism of children, responsibility of couples seeking marriage in the church and child protection issues. They have appointed a member of the congregation, Dr. Elizabeth McGavock, as designated person to provide consultation, advice and support with regard to child protection. Any matter which affects members meets with their interest. They know the people; they are of the people and, thus, they are able to maintain that unique Presbyterian characteristic of being ordained lay people working with the minister in the oversight of spiritual affairs. Theirs is a very daunting responsibility but they shoulder it with solemnity, diligence and humility.

THE CONGREGATIONAL COMMITTEE

The committee is the other elected body which helps to run the congregation. Its members deal with the practical and temporal aspects of church life. Their responsibilities include maintaining the church property in good condition, paying salaries and bills and ensuring that all day-to-day business is expedited with efficiency and in the best interests of the people.

The mammoth task of the first committee, with which this book deals, was to oversee the new church building project, a task which necessitated many long committee meetings and a great deal of thought and care. The members of that committee, elected in March 1973, were:-

> S. Alex Blair, John Boggs, Clarke Bashford, John Reid, William Christie, John Brown, Thompson

214

The Committee and Ladies' Committee which were responsible for overseeing the building and furnishing of the new Church.

Front row (left to right): Messrs. W.A. Tweed, A. McR. Brown, the Rev. R. McC. Bell, Mrs. J. Mathews, Mrs. W. Brown, Mrs. R. Bell, Mrs. J.R. McClure, Mrs. J. McIlhatton, Mrs. R. Patterson, the Rev. F.A. Robinson, Messrs. R. Patterson and W. Moore.

Middle row: Messrs. R.J. McClure, S. Tweed, A. McClure, W. Pinkerton, J. McClure, J. Wilson, J. Boggs, W. Carson, J. McClure, J. McQuiston, J. Reid, S.A. Blair, J. Brown, T. Elliott, T.A. Boyd, C. Bashford, J. McIlhatton, Jas. Richmond, J. Huey, W. Gault, W. Kirkpatrick, T. Lamont and R. Robinson.

Back row: Messrs. W. Christie, J. Lamont, R. Kerr, J. Mathews, Q. Robinson, J.R. McClure, W. Reid and J. Richmond. Not present for the picture: Dr. R.M. Kirkpatrick, R.A. Moore and A. Robinson

215

Elliott, William Gault, Joseph Lamont, Dr. R. Moore Kirkpatrick, James Huey, Robert Kerr, William Moore, Robert Moore, James McIlhatton, J. Richard McClure, Arnold McClure, John McClure, James McClure, James McQuiston, John Mathews, William Reid, William Pinkerton, Jack Richmond, James Richmond, Robert Patterson, Quentin Robinson, Alex. Robinson, Samuel Tweed, James Wilson.

Members of Kirk Session are ex-officio members of committee so it was a large team, augmented also by a committee of ladies, who planned the new church building, under the guidance of the Rev. Robin Bell and the architect, Mr. William Hunter.

After the church was opened, a new committee was elected in July 1976. Its members were:-

John Boggs, William Christie, James Huey, Robert Kerr, Joseph Lamont, J. Richard McClure, Frank McClure, James McClure, John McClure, James McQuiston, James T. McQuiston, John Mathews, Robert Moore, John Reid, William Reid, Bob Richmond, Geoffrey Robinson, Quentin Robinson, Samuel Tweed, James Wilson.

The Minute of a meeting of Kirk Session held on 14th July 1983 stated that:

"..votes by members of the congregation for fifteen members of congregational committee were counted."[26]

However the names of the fifteen elected are not recorded in either the Session or Committee Minute Books.

The next committee elected was in September 1988 and its members were:

Clarke Bashford, Maurice Christie, Joseph Guthrie, James Huey, Joseph Lamont, Carl McClure, Frank

McClure (Lisboy) Maurice McIntyre, James T. McQuiston, William Pinkerton, John Reid, Robert Richmond, Thomas Richmond, Geoffrey Robinson, Graham Robinson, Samuel Tweed.

Two stalwart members of committee from those days were Messrs J. Richard McClure, Churchview, and James McQuiston, Ballyveely. They were first elected in 1953 and gave over thirty years of service. Mr. McClure died on 4th May 1988 and Mr. McQuiston died on 12th October 1994. Mr. W. Arthur Tweed retired as secretary at a meeting on 6th February 1987. He was succeeded by Mr. J.A. Graham Robinson, who took up office on 2nd March 1987. Mr. Robinson resigned due to ill health in January 1999 and was succeeded by the present secretary Mr. Maurice F.R. Christie. The treasurer throughout the whole period with which this book deals has been Mr. Robert Patterson. He has given outstanding service to the church in this and many other capacities and the congregation owes him immense gratitude for a life time of work on their behalf.

The last congregational committee of Mr. Bell's ministry was elected in September 1991. Those elected were:-

Alex. Adair, Frank Archibald, Clarke Bashford, Jim Buick, Maurice Christie, Miss Lilian Elliott, Joseph Guthrie, Joseph Kirk, Frank McClure (Lisboy), John McClure, Mrs. Lorna McClure, Mrs. Charlotte McIlhatton, Maurice McIntyre, David McMullan, Robert McMullan, James T. McQuiston, William Pinkerton, Mrs. Janette Reid, John Reid, Tom Richmond and Geoffrey Robinson.

This was the first time in the congregation's history that ladies had been elected and Mr. Bell greeted this as "an historic moment"[27] for First Kilraughts.

There was one election for committee during the ministry of

The Committee, 2010.
Front row (left to right): Mrs. Charlotte McIlhatton, Miss Lilian Elliott, Mr. Maurice Christie (secretary), the Rev. Noel McClean, Mr. Robert Patterson (treasurer), Mrs. Lorna McClure, Mrs. Betty Robinson and Mrs. Janette Reid. Back row: Messrs. Sam McClure, James Morrison, Tom Richmond, Jim Murray, Frank McClure, Alan Pinkerton, Desi Nevin, Derek Brogan, Frank Archibald, Alex. Crawford and Miles Kelly

the Rev. David H. Thompson. It took place in June 1999 and those elected were:

Alex. Adair, Frank Archibald, Raymond Carson, Alex. Crawford, Lillian Elliott, Joseph Guthrie, Jim Murray, (Kilraughts), Frank McClure, (Lisboy), Lorna McClure, Lottie McIlhatton, Robert McMullan, James McQuiston, Desmond Nevin, Alan Pinkerton, Janette Reid, Tom Richmond, Betty Robinson, Geoffrey Robinson, Tom Skelton and William Tweed.

The present committee was elected in March 2006 and its members are:

Alex. Adair, Frank Archibald, Derek Brogan, Alex. Crawford, Lilian Elliott, Miles Kelly, Frank McClure (Lisboy), Lorna McClure, Sam McClure, Charlotte McIlhatton, James McQuiston, James Morrison, Jim Murray (Kilraughts), Desmond Nevin, Alan Pinkerton, Tom Richmond, Janette Reid, Tom Skelton and William Tweed.

They share, with the Kirk Session and minister, much of the responsibility for the celebrations of the 350th Anniversary year and are the publishers of this book.

Chapter 6

Notes and References

1. "Kilraughts: a Kirk and Its People", S.A. Blair, 1973 p171.
2. Memorial Minute, May 1973.
3. Letter from Miss Marjorie Gamble, included in Kirk Session Minutes, 1974.
4. "The Chronicle", 3rd April 1976.
5. See Obituary in "The Chronicle", 21st July 1984.
6. Minute of Meeting of Kirk Session, 12th June 1985.
7. Minute of Meeting of Kirk Session, 30th July 1985.
8. Minute of Meeting of Kirk Session, 30th September 1986.
9. Minute of Meeting of Kirk Session, 11th December 1986.
10. Ibid.
11. Minute of Meeting of Kirk Session, 25th January 1987.
12. Minute of Meeting of Kirk Session, 5th May 1988.
13. Ibid.
14. "Northern Constitution", 28th October 1989.
15. Minute of Meeting of Kirk Session, 26th May 1995.
16. Minute of Meeting of Kirk Session, 29th April 1997.
17. Memorial Minute of Kirk Session, passed at Session Meeting, 29th May 1998.
18. Memorial Minute of Kirk Session, passed at Session Meeting, 28th May 1999.
19. Memorial Minute of Kirk Session, passed at Session Meeting, 19th August 1999.
20. Minute Meeting of Kirk Session, 28th October 2000.
21. Minute of Meeting of Kirk Session, 10th February, 2002.
22. Minute of Meeting of Kirk Session, 8th November 2000.
23. Minute of Meeting of Kirk Session, 4th December 2005.
24. Minute of Meeting of Kirk Session, 29th October 2009.
25. Ibid.
26. Minute of Meeting of Kirk Session, 14th July 1983.
27. Minute of Meeting of Kirk Session, 30th September 1991.

Chapter 7

ORGANISATIONS

To the work of Minister, Kirk Session and Committee must be added the work of the various organisations, if any adequate picture of congregational life is to be given. First Kilraughts is fortunate in having a wide range of organisations catering for different age groups and interests and providing inspiration and recreation for the members.

MORNING SUNDAY SCHOOL

The opening of the Church Hall (now named the Robinson Hall) enabled a Morning Sunday School to be held. The Rev. F.A. Robinson was superintendent until May 1970 when the present author succeeded him.

As has already been recorded in Chapter 2, the pupils, by operating a talent scheme, raised in excess of the amount required to pay for a Sunday School window in the new church in 1975.

After the death of Reserve Constable John W. Moore, R.U.C., in a terrorist outrage in April 1978 (See Chapter 3) the John W. Moore Memorial Fund was set up. The Morning Sunday School benefited generously from this and John W. Moore Memorial Prizes were presented annually for creative work produced by the pupils. The first year in which these were awarded was 1980 and pupils were asked to interpret some topic which they had discussed in Sunday School. They could do this using writing, music or art and the pupils rose to the task, for the material which resulted left those who judged the entries very impressed indeed. In gave Sunday School work a new dimension and the displays of the entries attracted much interest in the congregation.

In November 2005 the award of these prizes was discontinued and the money was instead used to purchase teaching materials for the Sunday School. However it was made clear that the

The Morning Sunday School photographed in June 1996 when a retirement presentation was made to the Rev. R. McC. Bell

name of the John W. Moore Memorial Fund would be referred to each year at the June Sunday School Service.

A number of teachers have been honoured for their work in the Sunday School. In December 1978 Mr. Andrew McR. Brown was presented with a Bible when he retired after teaching for over twenty years. In April 1990 the superintendent, Mr. Blair, was made a presentation of two water colour paintings by Jack Wilkinson. They depicted the old and new churches and were the gift of the teachers and pupils in recognition of over thirty years as teacher and twenty years as superintendent. In April 1999 Mr. Blair was presented with a Bible from the Presbyterian Church in Ireland to commemorate forty years of teaching. Miss Margaret Kennedy received a similar Bible when she retired in September 2002 after thirty-five years as a teacher. She was also the guest at a dinner held by her colleagues in her honour.

Miss Margaret Kennedy receives flowers from Miss Lilian Elliott when she retired in September, 2002, after thirty-five years as a teacher in the Sunday School. Other teachers in the group are (left to right): Mrs. Michele McClean, Mr. Carl McClure (superintendent), Mr. Maurice Christie, the Rev. Noel McClean and Miss Regina McClure

The Sunday School Choir, June 2008

In the days when there were Afternoon Sunday Schools, the Morning Sunday School at the church functioned from the first Sunday in October to the last Sunday in April. In more recent years it has continued on to June and it includes a Bible Class, taken by the minister.

Each year the pupils enthusiastically participate in the Sunday School project of the Presbyterian Church in Ireland. They have visiting speakers from time to time and the Sunday School choir takes part in the Christmas Carol Service each year. Children's Day has been re-named as the day of special Sunday School services and members participate in the morning and evening services by leading the praise in a Sunday School choir and taking part in the readings and prayers.

The Sunday School party each December used to be the highlight of the year but by the 1990's it became clear that pupils preferred an outing and this has taken place annually since then.

The Sunday School, 2010. Back row (left to right): Carl McClure, Margaret McClure, Gemma McClean, the Rev. Noel McClean, Adam Brogan, Harry Walsh, Holly Clark, Emma McCook, Hannah Johnston, Danielle McNeill, Kerry Craig, Amy McMullan, Lilian Elliott, Marcus McClean, Charis McClean, Mark Lightbody, Regina McClure and Maurice Christie.

Middle row: Rachael Lightbody, Peter Craig, Thomas Clark, Ian Pinkerton, Rebecca Lightbody, Lydia Walsh, Amy Craig, Sarah Christie, Chloe McNeill, Charlotte Clark, Sandra Crawford and Alex. McNeill.

Front row: Aaron Fleming, Mark Crawford, Mark Brogan, Andrew McKay, Adam Dowey, Emma Pinkerton, Robert Dowey, Lewis Fleming, Evan Johnston, and Thomas Kelly.

225

Mr. Blair retired as superintendent in 1999 and was succeeded by Mr. Carl McClure. Mr. McClure with Miss Lilian Elliott and Mr. Maurice Christie have given many years of devoted service to the Morning Sunday School. In 2010 there are forty pupils on the Sunday School roll and seven teachers.

THE CHOIR AND CHOIR LEADERS

Praise has always held an important place in Presbyterian worship. In First Kilraughts there is a strong choir and a fine Cosgrove pipe organ to lead the praise at each service.

Miss Carmen Hanna (Mrs Michael) retired as organist at the end of April 1973 and she was succeeded by Mrs. Betty Caldwell who, as we have seen in Chapter 2, was ill during the ceremonies of the opening and dedication of the new church. She retired in July 1975 and Mr. Howard Gillespie, who had been organist from 1968-71, came back again and remained until April 1978. There was great difficulty in finding a suitable successor and Mrs. Caldwell kindly agreed to return until an appointment was made. Eventually Mrs. Eleanor Christie took on the position, but only in a temporary capacity, and she later said she could not continue after 25th February 1979. The Rev. Robin Bell then approached a young man in the congregation, Mr. Maurice Christie, and asked him if he would play at a Boys' Brigade Enrolement Service in December 1979. Maurice was in the B.B. and, after some hesitation, agreed. He was then invited to play at morning service and acquitted himself so well that Mr. Bell realised he had a very talented musician and an organist of much potential in the congregation. Maurice started playing regularly and the Session Minute Book records that by March 1980

> "…Mr. Maurice Christie is playing the organ and leading the praise with much acceptance."[1]

On 29th May 2005 a presentation was made to him to celebrate twenty-five years as organist of the congregation and

Mr. Marice Christie was the recipient of gifts on 29th May, 2005, when he completed twenty-five years as organist and choir leader. Mr. Robert Patterson, treasurer, made the presentation on behalf of the Church and also included are Mr. Arnold McClure, Clerk of Session (left), and the Rev. Noel McClean

Mr. Christie continues this most responsible work with great skill and enthusiasm.

On 21st October 1998 five members of the choir were the recipients of gifts in recognition of the fact that they had each given many years of dedicated service. They were Mrs. Charlotte McIlhatton (52 years); Mr. William Pinkerton (48 years); Miss Anne Kirkpatrick (45 years); Mrs. Grace Lamont (33 years) and Miss Lilian Elliott (29 years). Previous to that, on 15th October 1997, Miss Matilda Robinson was honoured for her many years in the choir and, on 21st December 2008, Mrs. McIlhatton was again the recipient of a gift when she completed sixty years in the choir.

The choir renders special music at times like Christmas and Easter and takes a leading part in the Carol Service each December. On these special occasions a group of talented

Miss Matilda Robinson was honoured on 15th October, 1997, for her many years of service in the choir. Included are (left to right): The Rev. David H. Thompson, Mrs. Angela Thompson, Mrs. Charlotte McIlhatton, who made the presentation, Mr. Maurice Christie, organist and choir leader, Miss Matilda Robinson, Mrs. Roseanne Bell and the Rev. Robin Bell

Five members were honoured with gifts on 21st October, 1998, for their years of service to the Church choir. They are (standing, left to right): Mrs. Grace Lamont (33 years), Miss Anne Kirkpatrick (45 years), Mr. William Pinkerton (48 years), Mrs. Charlotte McIlhatton (52 years) and Miss Lilian Elliott (29 years). Seated are the Rev. R. McC. Bell, Mr. Maurice Christie, Organist and the Rev. D.H. Thompson

228

The Choir in 1996 when they presented gifts to the Rev. Robin and Mrs. Roseanne Bell at the time of Mr. Bell's retirement

Mrs. Charlotte McIlhatton receives gifts and congratulations on 21st December, 2008, when she completed sixty years in the choir. With her are Mr. Maurice Christie, organist and choir leader and Miss Lilian Elliott, another long-standing member of the choir, who made the presentations

young musicians often play and their contributions are enjoyed and appreciated also. A highlight of the year is the annual Praise Service, which is organised by the choir and organist, and has been taking place since 1976. Some well-known choirs have taken part:

Year	Choir	Conductor
1976	Ballymoney & District Male Voice Choir	Terry McNeilly
1977	Ballywatt Presbyterian Church Choir	Roberta Scott
1978	West Church (B/Mena) Presbyterian Church Choir	William Livingstone
1979	St. James's Presbyterian Church Choir	Cecil Thompson
1980	Route Presbytery Choral Festival	James Moore
1981	The Laggan Choir, Donegal	Mary McSparren
1982	The Route Singers	Howard Gillespie
1983	McQuiston Memorial Presbyterian Church Choir	Ronald McCully
1984	Downshire Ladies Choir	William Thompson
1985	Ballyclare Male Voice Choir	William Thompson
1986	Ballymoney & District Male Voice Choir	Alex. Gillen
1987	The Laggan Choir, Donegal	Mary McSparren
1988	The Route Singers	Howard Gillespie
1989	The Seven Towers Male Voice Choir	Elizabeth Strahan

The Church Choir, 2010. Front row (left to right): Lilian Elliott, Valerie Tweed, Nichola Hegarty, Charis McClean, Rachael Lightbody. Second row: Lyndsey Hegarty, Angela McClure, Anne Kirkpatrick, Mae Crawford, Grace Lamont, Mary McClure. Third Row: Elizabeth Jane Kelly, Tracey Murray, Janette Reid, Elizabeth McMillan, Louise Glenn, Anne Murray, Charlotte McIlhatton. Back row: Steven Glenn, Samuel Tweed, Arnold McClure, David McMillan, Ian McClure, Maurice Christie

1990	Belmont Presbyterian Church Choir	John Mercer
1991	St. James's Presbyterian Church Choir	Cecil Thompson
1992	Bushmills Male Voice Choir	Lynda Elliott
1993	Ballymena Presbytery Choir	Rev. R.E. Harry Uprichard
1994	Ballymoney & District Male Voice Choir	Alex. Gillen
1995	Dalriada School Junior Choir	Heather Montgomery
1996	The Seven Towers Male Voice Choir	Thelma Strange
1997	The Foyle Presbytery Choir	Rev. Dr. Ivan Wilson

1998	Ballymena Presbytery Choir	Rev. R.E. Harry Uprichard
1999	Dalriada School Junior & Chamber Choirs	Heather Montgomery
2000	The Route Singers	Howard Gillespie
2001	No Praise Service held due to foot & mouth restrictions	
2002	Ballymoney High School Choir	Glynis Church
2003	Ballymena Academy Chamber Choir	Paul McQueen
2004	The Route Singers	Margaret Brown
2005	Donegal Presbytery Choir	Trevor Gamble
2006	Ballyclare Male Voice Choir	Brian Angus
2007	Ballycastle High School Choir	Lorna Palmer
2008	The Boys' Brigade Centenary Male Voice Choir	Yvette Anderson
2009	Ballymena Presbytery Male Voice Choir	Tom McNeill
2010	Harlandic Male Voice Choir	John Lyttle

The Moderator of the General Assembly is usually the guest preacher at these services and they attract large numbers of visitors from near and far.

SUNDAY MORNING PRAYER GROUP

This began in 2008 and meets in the Session Room before the morning service on the second and fourth Sundays of the month. In "1st K. Kirk News" in December 2009 the Rev. Noel McClean wrote that he feels this meeting..

> "...certainly brings blessing on a congregation and is much appreciated by the minister as he enters the pulpit. Thank you to those who attend our prayer meeting. It

may not have been a tradition in North Antrim, unlike other places; but as the poet Tennyson said; 'more things are wrought by prayer than this world dreams of.'"[2]

CRECHE

A crèche is available in the Robinson Hall each Sunday for pre-school children. Parents are then free, having left their children in the crèche, to take part in the service of worship. This has been much appreciated over the years and is staffed by sympathetic, patient and experienced leaders.

CHILDREN'S CHURCH

After the children's address, the young children leave for their own Children's Church in the Circular Room. Leaders engage them in Bible stories and use a variety of activities including singing, drama, craft, drawing and games to retain the children's interest and bring the stories to life.

Children's Church takes place every Sunday and has a very dedicated and trusted team of leaders.

CRAIGATEMPIN AFTERNOON SUNDAY SCHOOL

When the period under review in this book begins there was only one Afternoon Sunday School operating within the bounds of the congregation. It was at Craigatempin Hall and had been started in 1888. Originally, it had met every Sunday at 3pm but by the 1970's it only met during the summer months. Mr. Thomas Tweed was superintendent from 1955 to 1972 and his successor was Mr. Thomas Lamont, who held the position until 1983. (For more on these two men, see Chapter 6).

Mr. Desmond Hill became superintendent in 1983 and it was during his time in position that the Centenary of the Sunday School was celebrated. There was always a special anniversary service held each year on the first Sunday in June and in June 1988 the Centenary Service was held. Two moderators attended

Those who took part in the Centenary Service at Craigatempin Hall in June, 1988. The Rt. Rev. Dr. William Fleming, Moderator of the General Assembly is seated and standing (left to right) are: The Rev. R. McC. Bell, the Rev. Professor Adam Loughridge, Moderator of Synod of the R.P. Church, Mr. S. Alex Blair and the Sunday School Superintendent, Mr. Demond Hill

– the Moderator of the Presbyterian Church in Ireland, the Rt. Rev. Dr. William Fleming, who preached, and the Rev. Professor Adam Loughridge, Moderator of the Synod of the Reformed Presbyterian Church, who read from the scriptures and prayed. Dr. Loughridge also recalled his connection with Craigatempin over the years, saying he had, as a boy, come to "preachings" in the Hall and had preached there himself often in later years. The present author gave a short account of the history of the Sunday School and the service was conducted by the Rev. Robin Bell. A warm welcome was extended to the large gathering by the superintendent, Mr. Desmond Hill. One of the teachers, Miss Anne McC Kirkpatrick, was presented with a Bible by Dr. Fleming, the gift of the Presbyterian Church in

Ireland in recognition of forty years of service as a teacher in Craigatempin.

Although there were satisfactory numbers of young people attending at that time, the next decade saw a dramatic decline and in 1998 the Trustees had, reluctantly, to close the school and sell the hall. At a meeting of First Kilraughts Church Committee in January 2004 it was recorded that Craigatempin Hall had been sold, but it was made clear that...

> "...the sale of the hall was under the control of the Trustees of the hall and not First Kilraughts Presbyterian Church committee."[3]

Nevertheless, First Kilraughts Morning Sunday School and other youth work in the congregation benefitted considerably from the money realised by the sale.

YOUTH FELLOWSHIP

On the evening of Sunday, 30th April 1990 the Rev. Robin Bell held a meeting with the aim of establishing a Youth Fellowship in First Kilraughts. The meeting was addressed by the Rev. John T. McCullough, minister of Toberdoney and Croaghmore, who had much experience in working with youth groups. Three elders were present and the Session Minute Book recorded:

> "There was much interest among the young people and, to retain the momentum, it was decided to hold a meeting on a Sunday evening in July and August, before commencing regular meetings in September.

> Mr. Graham Robinson suggested that a note should be prepared giving details of the Youth Fellowship. This could be distributed by elders when visiting prior to communion.

Subsequently Mr. Robinson produced a note which gave the aim of the organization as:

The Youth Fellowship, 2010. Front row (left to right): Harry Walsh, Sandra Crawford, Adam Brogan. Second row: Nichola Hegarty, Charis McClean, Gemma McClean, Marcus McClean. Third row: Rachael Lightbody, Lyndsay Hegarty, Alison Robinson, Louise Glenn, Emily Walsh. Back row: Mark Lightbody, Tracey Murray, the Rev. Noel McClean, Chris Hogg, Maurice Christie, Steven Glenn

> 'To win and to strengthen young people for Jesus Christ within an informal fellowship as part of the church family.'

> Elders agreed to distribute this at their discretion."[4]

Thus, the foundations were laid and many young people have been involved in the Youth Fellowship down the years since 1990.

The Rev. Noel McClean has commented:

> "The Youth Fellowship unites young people in a happy Christian environment where they can discuss, share and grow in their Christian faith. The Sunday night

meetings have a variety of speakers and topics relevant to those who attend, and the leaders, past and present, have a real burden for the young people to enable them to find faith and strengthen their faith for the pressures that teenagers face today. We realise that the world our young people live in now is very different from that of 30 years ago and thus we see this organisation as one of the most important in our church and are anxious that all our young people benefit from it and cement the friendships they have with each other."[5]

As well as monthly meetings on a Sunday evening, activities also include a number of Saturday night social gatherings for fun and fellowship and the annual "Weekend Away" in September is much enjoyed. In recent years an annual church service has been part of the programme, with members taking part and benefitting from a guest speaker.

The Youth Fellowship is seen as an important organisation which strengthens youth in the church and augers well for the future. It is important to realise that these young people are the leaders of the next generation.

THE SUNDAY EVENING FELLOWSHIP

The Bible Study Group was established during the ministry of the Rev. Robin Bell and continued under the Rev. David Thompson as the Sunday Evening Fellowship. Usually at the meetings a passage of scripture was studied in some detail and members were invited to participate in discussion.

Under the Rev. Noel McClean the scope of these meetings has been broadened. In some sessions a particular Biblical book, topic or passage is highlighted, led by the minister, and in others there are guest speakers who deal with issues of interest. The meetings are informal, take place in the Circular Room, and are held on the first and third Sunday evenings of the winter months.

MISSIONARY PRAYER GROUP

In the Manse and in homes of various members a small group have come together since 2008 to pray for missionary causes and personnel. They meet on the last Tuesday of each month, excluding the summer months.

PRESBYTERIAN WOMEN (THE P.W.)

Presbyterian Women is a new name, given on 1st May 2008, to the oldest organisation associated with First Kilraughts. The link goes back, through its original name, the Women's Missionary Association, to the 1890's. At the instigation of the Rev. John McCammon, little wooden mission boxes were given out to every household in the congregation and the "woman of the house" was asked to fill the box with change as she saw fit. At the end of each year there was a Mission Box Opening Night, presided over by Mrs. D. J. MacMaster, Topp, when the women brought their boxes to the church and the money was counted. It was then sent off to augment W.M.A. funds and help support the Presbyterian missionaries.

In 1934 Mrs. F.A. Robinson decided regular meetings should be held and these were given strong support by the women of the congregation. So the meetings have continued ever since, now taking place every second Tuesday night of the month from September through to March.

The organisation's name was changed in 1971 to the Presbyterian Women's Association (P.W.A.) and, when the new church was opened in 1975, First Kilraughts P.W.A. presented the four beautiful plate glass windows in the Circular Room which have on them an engraved depiction of the 23rd Psalm. The P.W.A. was also responsible for a catering programme for visiting groups and organisations which raised large sums of money for the Church Building Fund.

In 2004 the seventieth anniversary of First Kilraughts P.W.A.

was celebrated with the production of a Peter Stanier Fine Bone China Mug depicting the church and a special cake was baked for the occasion. Each year a lunch is provided for the senior members of the congregation at Christmas and the annual "fund raiser" is a Spring Tea held at Easter time. The year ends with a service in church on the first Sunday in May. There is always a special speaker and members conduct the service.

The cake which was part of the 70th Anniversary Celebrations of the Kilraughts P.W.A., 2004

The organisation's aim has been the same throughout its long history – to support the missionaries of the church with gifts of time, money and prayers and to unite the women of the church in the dedication of their lives to Jesus Christ. The Motto of the P.W. is "Living for Jesus" and its Mission Statement says it encourages women to become disciples of Christ. The P.W. aims to highlight the need for:

∑ Love and Unity

∑ Obedience to God

∑ Christian Living and Spiritual maturity

First Kilraughts P.W., 2010.

Back row (left to right): Mrs. Jeanette Reid, Mrs. Lila Munnis, Miss Anne Kirkpatrick, Mrs. Jennifer Reid, Mrs. Stephanie Hunter, Mrs. Valerie Tweed, Mrs. Elizabeth Jane Kelly, Mrs. Annie Patterson, Mrs. Angela McClure, Mrs. Anne Richmond, Miss Lilian Elliott, Mrs. Norma McClure, Mrs. Linda Crawford, Mrs. Lorna McClure.
Middle row: Mrs. Lottie McIlhatton, Mrs. Mae Crawford, Mrs. Claire Brogan, Mrs. Anne Murray, Mrs. Gloria McClure, Mrs. Ruby Christie, Mrs. Eleanor Huey, Miss Margaret Kennedy, Mrs. Grace Lamont, Mrs. Annie Kirk, Mrs. Mary Murray, Mrs. Betty Robinson.
Front row: Mrs. Ruth Gracey, Miss Kathleen McClure, Mrs. Peggy Tweed, Mrs. Betha McClure, Mrs. Michele McClean, Mrs. Inez Richmond, Mrs. Mary McClure, Mrs. Sarah Brown, Mrs. Linda Pinkerton, Mrs. Annie Reid

$\sum$ Service using gifts, time and money.

$\sum$ Local and Global Mission

The P.W. is well supported in First Kilraughts and plays a vibrant part in congregational life.

THE BOYS' BRIGADE

On the evening of Sunday, 30th November 1975 the Second Route Company of the Boys' Brigade was re-constituted in First Kilraughts Church after having been in abeyance for a quarter of a century. Thirty-six boys, half in the Junior Section, and the other half in the Company Section, were enrolled at the special service, conducted by the Rev. R. McC. Bell, minister, and chaplain of the company. B.B. officers from other companies in the Route Presbytery attended, together with a congregation of about two hundred parents and friends. Officers of the new company commissioned were –

Captain: Geoffrey Robinson

Lieutenants: Mae Crawford, Robert Moore, Maurice McIntyre and James McClure

Geoffrey Robinson has remained captain and has given most dedicated leadership down the years. He can recall the 18 young men in the Company Section in 1975. They were:

Squad 1 Alex. Millar, Raymond Cushnahan, James Linton, Gary Connolly, Richard McCook and David Connolly.

Squad 2 Paul Christie, Colin Kirkpatrick, Alan Brown, Alex. Crawford, Alan Pinkerton and Martin Christie.

Squad 3 Thomas Millar, Kenneth Murphy, Kim Kirkpatrick, Colin Christie, Alan Wilson (deceased) and Alan Connolly.

Two years after the re-constitution of the Junior and Company Sections, the Anchor Boys were formed (1977), and have attracted strong support ever since.

The Re-Constituted 2nd Route Company of the Boys' Brigade, 1976
Back row (left to right): Mae Crawford, James McClure, Robert Petticrew,
David Connolly, Paul Christie, Alan Brown, Colin Kirkpatrick, James
Linton, Maurice McIntyre, Noeleen McQuiston.
Third row: Alan Connolly, Alan Pinkerton, Raymond Cushnahan, Gary
Connolly, Alex. Crawford, Geoffrey Robinson, Rev. Robin Bell, Robert
McPherson (Inspecting Officer), Robert Moore, Kenneth Murphy, Martin
Christie, Colin Christie, Richard McCooke, Kim Kirkpatrick.
Front row: Cecil Linton, Jeffrey Walker, Robin Crawford, Ivor Buick, Derek
Cushnahan, Leonard Linton, Andrew McQuiston

During the Centenary Year of the Boys Brigade in 1983 the company attended a Celebratory Day in Ballymoney when Lord Elgin K.T., International President of the BB, hosted the day and cut the celebration cake. That was the beginning of a whole series of important events in which the Second Route Company was involved. On 2nd July 1983, Alan McLean, with the captain, Geoffrey Robinson, attended the Royal Review Parade at Holyrood Palace, Edinburgh, when five hundred boys were reviewed by H.M. the Queen in a horse-drawn open carriage. The Captain also attended the Centennial Camp at Mystery Creek near Hamilton, North Island, New Zealand, which was attended by some 1,900 boys and officers from many

In the Centenary Year of the Boys' Brigade, 1983, the Mayor of North Down, the Rev. J. McConnell Auld, inspects the Company Section at the Annual Display. With him is the Captain, Geoffrey Robinson

Cutting the cake to mark twenty-five years of the B.B. in Kilraughts as the re-constituted 2nd Route Company. Included are (left to right): the Rev. Robin and Mrs. Roseanne Bell, the Captain Geoffrey Robinson and Mrs. Angela Thompson and the Rev. David Thompson

At B.B. Camp, 1988. Included are (left to right): Geoffrey Robinson, James McClure, Keith Thompson, Philip Linton, Mark McClure, Jonathan McClure, Mark Thompson, Colin Richmond, Robert McMullan and Alan Pinkerton

parts of the world. The Second Route Company took part in an event nearer home when they participated in a parade and service of thanksgiving held in St. Anne's Cathedral, Belfast, on Sunday, 9th October 1983. At home in Kilraughts, the Rev. Robin Bell planted a Japanese Maple (Malius Sargentii) in the grounds of the church to commemorate the Centenary.

On 26th January 1981 the Company Section came first in the Route Battalion Drill competition and 5th in the Northern Ireland district competition. On Saturday 12th June 1993 the 2nd Route Junior Section attended a 75th anniversary Fun Day at B.B. Recreation Centre, Belvoir, Belfast.

A highlight of the year has always been the Annual Camp, the first of which was held from 20th-24th July 1976 at Tullymore Forest Park. The cost for each boy was £7. Over the years camps have been held at a great variety of venues in Northern Ireland, as well as in Scotland, England and the Isle of Man.

The Queen's Badge is the highest award in the Boys Brigade. The following boys have received this award in Second Route Company:

1981	Alex. Crawford, Alan Pinkerton
1982	Maurice Christie, Robin Crawford
1983	Alan McLean
1992	John Christie
1993	James Buick, Richard Richmond
199	Philip Christie, Mark Murray
1997	Paul Fleming, Steven Reid (presented with their certificates at Queen's University by Paul Clarke, the T.V. Newsreader.)
2005	Andrew Morrison, Philip Thompson
2009	Thomas Skelton, Andrew Reid

In September 2009 Thomas Skelton also received the King George VI Officer Cadet Training Award. This enables the recipient to receive training for leadership and provides an opportunity to learn new skills, make new friends, explore his faith and grow in confidence. Thomas is the only boy in the company, so far, to have gained this very prestigious award.

At the weekly meetings on Monday evenings "turn-out", discipline and behaviour are marked, Christian Education classes are held and there are different badges to be worked for including cookery, craftwork, drill, first aid and safety. P.E. forms part of the programme and there is 5-a-side football and a great range of activities for the boys to enjoy.

The officers in 2010 are: Geoffrey Robinson (Captain), Tom

Two members of the 2nd Route Company were presented with their Queen's Badge Certificates by Paul Clarke, television personality, on 24th September, 1997. They where Steven Reid and Paul Fleming. With them is the Captain, Geoffrey Robinson

Thomas Skelton who, in 2009, won the Queen's Badge and the King George VI Officer Cadet Training Award

2nd Route Company B.B. Anchor Boys, 2010
Back row (left to right0; Mrs. Jennie Reid, Rev. Noel McClean, Mrs. Claire
Brogan, Miss Charis McClean. Middle row: Adam Dowey, Andrew McKay,
Aaron Fleming, Jonathan Kirk, Adam Walker, Zachariah Logan, Mark
Brogan, Andrew Boyd, Ben Bartlett, Lewis Fleming, John Boyd. Front row:
Harry Orr, Sam Lowry, Robert Dowey, Carlon Bartlett

2nd Route Company B.B. Junior Section, 2010
Back row (left to right): Mrs. Michele McClean, Rev. Noel McClean, Mr.
Miles Kelly. Middle row: Owen Farrell, Graham Bartlett, Tom Lowry,
Philip Bellingham, Adam Quinn, Daniel Logan. Front row: Mark
Crawford, Thomas Clark, Oliver Watt, Peter Craig, Ian Pinkerton

2nd Route Company B.B. Company Section, 2010
Front row (left to right): Rev. N. McClean, Pte. Peter Kerr, Pte. Harry
Walsh, Pte. Adam Brogan, Pte. Tom Boreland, Lieut. Tom Skelton.
Middle row: W/O. Allan McCook, Pte. Jack Calderwood, Pte. Ross Kerr,
Pte. James Reid.
Back row: Lieut. Alan Pinkerton, L/Cpl. Marcus McClean, Sgt. Andrew
Skelton, L/Cpl. Adam Kerr, L/Cpl. John Brown, L/Cpl. Daniel McCord,
Geoffrey Robinson (Captain)

Skelton, Alan Pinkerton, Michele McClean, Jenny Reid, and Claire Brogan with Alan McCook, Miles Kelly and Charis McClean (helpers)

GUIDES, BROWNIES AND RAINBOWS

First Kilraughts Brownies started in 1975 and was for girls aged 7 to 10 years. The first Guider/Brown Owl was Margaret Moore assisted by Tawny Owl Margaret Murray. The Brownies met on Friday evenings and continue to do so. Warranted Brownie Guiders down the years, in addition to Margaret Moore and Margaret Murray, have included Roseanne Bell,

Diane Louden, Regina McClure and the present Guider, Wilma Skelton.

The Rainbows began in 1987 and their age range is 4 to 7 years. Roseanne Bell was Guider, assisted by Diane Louden. Other Warranted Rainbow Guiders have included Mary Murray, Debi Logan, Louise Clarke and Regina McClure, who is the present Guider.

The Guides began in First Kilraughts in 2003 for girls 10 to 14 years. Prior to this, girls, when they reached 10 years, had to join the Guide Company in Ballymoney. Debi Logan was the first Guider and the present Guider is Heather McCook.

Personal development and achievement are the key aims of Guiding and girls and young women are encouraged to:

Σ Develop as individuals.

Σ Develop positive attitudes.

Σ Share and develop skills, interests and talents.

Σ Be flexible.

Σ Be challenged to learn new skills.

Σ Be encouraged to learn about the local and wider community.

Girls and young women have the freedom and the opportunity to:

Σ Decide on activities they all enjoy.

Σ Work together in teams.

Σ Interact with each other on an equal basis.

Σ Assert themselves.

Σ See other women in positions of responsibility and taking the lead.

Σ Develop a sense of identity and self-worth.

First Kilraughts Rainbows, Brownies and Guides celebrating the Centenary of Guiding, 2010.
Front: Holly Clark, Anna Boreland. Rainbows: Molly Porterfield, Eve Borland, Charlotte Lynn, Faith McAfee, Callie Thompson, Emma Pinkerton, Kerry Jamison. Brownies: Courtney Craig, Lydia Walsh, Cerys Bartlett, Ellis Thompson, Nicola Gault, Alex McNeill, Georgia McDonald. Guides: Charlotte Clark, Alice Skelton, Amy Craig, Sandra Crawford, Emma McCook, Jodie McBride, Emma McKeeman, Victoria Horrigan. Guiders: Wilma Skelton, Regina McClure, Heather McCook, Emma Richmond, Jackie McBride

The Guiding Method is made up of the Five Essentials and applies to all sections:

∑ Girls work together in small groups.

∑ Girls are encouraged to govern themselves and make their own decisions.

∑ Girls have a balanced and varied programme.

∑ Girls care for the individual.

∑ Girls share a commitment to a common standard.

Guides, Brownies and Rainbows at First Kilraughts work through varied programmes which include craft, cookery, drama, quizzes, informative visits, various outings, church services and sleepovers. They hold fundraisers and have an annual Parents and Friends evening at the end of the year.

Guides work towards "go-for-its". Brownies complete activity badges and Rainbows work through what is known as their four piece jigsaw.

2010 has been the Centenary Year of Guiding and it was launched on 5th September 2009 at the Giant's Causeway when 100 girls stood on 100 stones to represent each year of Guiding. The Celebrations, in which Kilraughts has been enthusiastically involved, concluded with a Grand Finale on 20th October 2010.

THE INDOOR BOWLING CLUB

The Indoor Bowling Club was formed in 1966 when the Rev. F.A. Robinson encouraged a number of enthusiasts led by Tom Boyd and John Henry to come together to enjoy the game. Mr. Robinson saw it as an asset to the congregation, bringing people together and giving them shared leisure in a pleasant environment.

The Club celebrated its 25th Anniversary with a service on 22nd September 1991, at which the special preacher was the Rev.

Presentation to Mr. and Mrs. Robert Patterson made by the Indoor Bowling Club in 1998. Mr. and Mrs. Patterson are seated and standing are (left to right): Mrs. Anne Richmond, Mr. James Louden, the Rev. David Thompson, Mr. William Moore and Mrs. Ruby Christie

William Hook, himself a keen bowler. In 1998 the Captain, Robert Patterson, and his wife Annie, were honoured with a presentation of a lamp and vase in Tyrone Crystal. Robert had been captain for 25 years and still continues his leadership as captain today. Annie had arranged the catering for home matches and many tributes were paid to their work for the club.

Kilraughts bowlers play friendly matches with neighbouring clubs. The only competitive bowls they play is in the E. T. Taylor Charity Cup and in doing so they have raised, through the years, considerable sums of money for the local branch of the Northern Ireland Hospice.

Although six months late, the club celebrated its 40th Anniversary with a Dinner and Prize Distribution in the Causeway Hotel in March 2007. The captain presented a special

First Kilraughts Indoor Bowling Club, 2010.

Front row (left to right): William Moore, Grace Lamont, Ruby Christie, Robert Patterson, Ann Richmond, Rev. Noel McClean, Arnold McClure. Second row: Betha McClure, Annie Kirk, Hannah Connolly, Pearl Stirling, Sam Connolly, James Louden, Desmond Hill, Joe Lamont, Joe Kirk. Back row: Mae Crawford, Isabell Moore, James Morrison, Robert Stirling, Ann Heron, Robert Moore, Dan Hanna, Lorna McClure, Annie Patterson cake decorated to resemble a bowling mat and a very enjoyable evening was held.

The club meets on Wednesday nights during the winter months, with some matches also being played on Thursday evenings.

THE BADMINTON CLUB

The Badminton Club was formed in the early years of the ministry of the Rev. F.A. Robinson by a number of enthusiastic badminton players led by Wallace Pinkerton. Teams were entered in the Ballymoney and Coleraine Leagues and friendly matches were played.

The club ceased to function for a time but started up again in the mid-1970's under the captaincy of Frank McClure, Lisboy. Frank is recorded as being "captain, coach and advisor" to the club and Mrs. Roseanne Bell was a keen player, becoming the club President. By 1983 there were 53 members and so much activity that premises had to be hired to facilitate all the matches in which the club was involved.

In November 1982 a junior club was formed for young people aged 8 to 15 years and it also met on a Friday evening, supervised by senior members. It had a membership of 30 in its first year. Later parental help was sought for supervision and Frank McClure, Kilraughts Road, took over the role of coaching the juniors.

The senior club lapsed for a few years but began again in 1993 with Miss Lilian Elliott as President. She and Carl McClure ran it jointly until 2005 when Desmond and Irene Nevin took over. Due to lack of interest, the club ceased in 2008.

THE YOUTH CLUB

When the Youth Club was formed during the ministry of the Rev. F.A. Robinson it was the biggest club in the congregation.

First Kilraughts Badminton Club in the 1980's

Front row (left to right): Cathern McMullan, Heather Louden, Lorna Lamont, Suzanne Watt, Fiona McNeill. Seated: Pamela Stinson, Sandra Neill, Valerie Lamont, Brenda Lamont, Mary Britton, Britton children, Heather Kerr, Irene McClure, Elaine McNeill, Lilian Elliott. Third Row: Brian Stinson, Noel Watt, Rae Torrens, Irene McLaughlin, Roseanne Bell, Valerie Brown, Ann McClure, Trevor Munnis, Carl McClure, James McClure (Blackhills). Back row: Billy Stevenson, Paddy McLaughlin, John Stewart, Frank McClure, jun., William Munnis, William Torrens, Fobin Neill, Chesney Britton, Arnold McClure, Frank McClure (Lisboy)

Nearly all the young people joined and they played badminton and table tennis, but not with the professional skills of those in the Badminton Club. They played for their own enjoyment.

It was the Youth Club which had the idea of holding a Grand Auction Sale to raise funds for the new church and it was an outstanding success. It took place in the church grounds on Saturday 19th June 1971 and attracted massive crowds, raising two thousand pounds to boost the Building Fund. The club also held concerts, dances, sponsored walks and was a most vibrant and enthusiastic group.

Because of all these efforts the club was in good financial footing and in 1973 the members decided to give Christmas gifts of peat briquettes or coal to elderly members of the church who lived alone. This was done for a number of years.

They expanded their activities with the purchase of a snooker table in 1978 and swimming became part of their programme with the opening of the Riada Centre in Ballymoney.

By 1980 membership began to fall and consideration was given as to whether the club should become part of the Badminton Club. However new members joined and by 1999 there were 30 club members.

Supervision was a great problem and, although parents helped, it became more and more difficult to comply with legislation and the Youth Club reluctantly closed.

THE G.F. ASSOCIATION

When, in 1974, the Presbyterian Church decided to discontinue the branches of the Girls' Auxiliary throughout the church, First Kilraughts wanted to keep their branch. It was agreed to do so under the new name of Girls' Fellowship and the first meeting took place in May 1975. Miss Lilian Elliott, who was the Girls' Auxiliary leader, continued in office and the motto and aims of the new organization were those of the Girls'

First Kilraughts Junior Girls' Fellowship, 1980

Front row (left to right): Lesley Brown, Michelle Mark, Janice Reid. Second row: Yvonne McCloskey, ___, Lorna Dowey, Hazel Johnston, Jacqueline McMullan. Back row: Lilian Elliott (leader), Mrs. Bell, Alex. Bell, Lorna Moore, Kathern Brown, Rosemary McClintock, Karen Wasson, Janice Buick, Rosemary McClintock, Karen Mark, Rev. Robin Bell, Margaret Murray (leader)

First Kilraughts G.F. – Senior Girls, 1980

Front row (left to right): Rosemary Moore, Jacqueline McCook, Fiona McNeill. Second row: Hazel Moore, Heather Brown, ___, Michelle Connolly, Betty Walker, Claire Dowey, Caroline Bell, Suzanne Watt. Back row: Lilian Elliot (leader), the Rev. Robin Bell, Valerie Glenn, Heather McCloskey, Linda Moore, Valerie Moore, Sandra Huey, Yvonne Simpson, Irene McClure, Mandy Dowey, Mrs. Roseanne Bell, Margaret Murray (leader)

First Kilraughts Girls' Fellowship Association, June 2010.
Front row (left to right): Anna McCluggage, Jessica McKay, Emma Pinkerton, Emma Dowey, Jenny McCluggage. Second row: Erin Caldwell, Hannah Kirk, Cerys Bartlett, Alana Caldwell. Third row: Charlotte Clark, Sarah Christie, Alex. McNeill, Chloe Gillan. Fourth row: Sandra Crawford, Erin Ramsey, Alice Skelton, Rebecca Lightbody, Emma Gillan, Chloe McNeill, Lydia Walsh, Courtney Craig. Back row: Rachel Lightbody (helper), Rachel Watt, Regina McClure (leader), Georgia Allen, Alison Walker (leader), E.J. Kelly (leader), Lilian Elliott (leader)

Auxiliary. Later the name was changed to the G.F. Association and the work was supported by a grant from the North-Eastern Education and Library Board.

Girls from 4 to 16 years of age enjoy the wide programme of activities each Friday evening during the summer months. Highlights down the years have included the annual sausage sizzle, the annual trip to the zoo and events like barbeques, treasure hunts, cycle rides to Ballycastle, visits to the swimming pool, a boat trip on Lough Neagh and a day at Carnfunnock Country Park, Larne.

To raise funds, the girls have organised family fun nights, table quizzes, a car wash, a one day shop and a balloon race. On 22nd August 1998 the girls released 400 balloons in the church car park and one travelled as far as Austria. At that time a former member of the G.F. was teaching English in Austria and she arranged to meet the young lady who found the Kilraughts G.F. Balloon. This gave all the girls and the leaders a great thrill.

On 9th August 2000 the G.F. celebrated its 25th Anniversary with a special service, conducted by the minister, the Rev. David Thompson. There is always a religious element to each of their meetings and they have a G.F. service in church each year.

CONCLUSION

To use a current phrase: "First Kilraughts is more than a Sunday service". It is a living, vital church, part of the local community and offering facilities and opportunities to that community. As we have seen in this concluding chapter, the church, as well as having its spiritual dimension, generates a great variety of activities and has much to offer. Many people willingly devote much time to these activities, and, as has been the case down the generations, they seek no reward. Their attitude and aspiration is put eloquently in this verse which depicts them as workers with each other and co-workers with God:

"And the work that we have builded,
Oft with bleeding hands and tears,
Oft in error, oft in anguish,
Will not perish with the years;
It will last and shine transfigured
In the final reign of right;
It will pass into the splendours
Of the City of the Light."

The work has been blessed in Kilraughts for three hundred and fifty years and, in confidence, the congregation looks forward to the years ahead.

Chapter 7

Notes and References

1. Minute of Meeting of Kirk Session, 14th March 1980
2. "1st K Kirk News", Vol 9,p7.
3. Minute Book of Committee, p317
4. Minute of Meeting of Kirk Session, 30th April 1990
5. Notes from Rev. Noel McClean to author, May 2010